MW00606023

OVERCOMING ROADBLOCKS TO HEALING

BY
MARK R. ANDERSON

OVERCOMING ROADBLOCKS TO HEALING
By Mark R. Anderson
www.markandersonministries.com
P.O. Box 66 Cody, WY 82414-0066 USA
Email: goodnews@vcn.com   Phone: 307-587-0408
© Copyright 2012–Mark Anderson Ministries

All rights reserved. This book is protected by the copyright laws of the United States of America. This book may not be copied or reprinted for commercial gain or profit. The use of short quotations or occasional page copying for personal or group study is permitted and encouraged. Permission will be granted upon request. Unless otherwise identified, Scripture quotations are from the New King James Version Copyright © 1982 by Thomas Nelson Inc. Used by permission. Scripture quotations marked AMP are taken from the Amplified® Bible, Copyright © 1954, 1958, 1962, 1964 1965, 1987 by The Lockman Foundation. Used by Permission. All rights reserved. Emphasis within Scripture quotations is author's own.

Published by: Apostolic Network of Global Awakening
1451 Clark St. Mechanicsburg, PA 17055 USA

Portions of the this book are taken from Mark R. Anderson's other books, *You can Tap into Christ's Healing Power* Published by © Mark Anderson Ministries 2004 and *Humility the Hidden Key to Walking in Signs and Wonders* published by © Destiny Image 2010.

Trade Paper ISBN: 978-1-9374-6712-8

Endorsements

"Mark Anderson knows what he is writing about. He has lived it and continues to preach the message of healing and freedom throughout the world. Here in this book he makes it simple and shows you how to bring healing into your own life. This is a great contribution to the Body of Christ..."

-Harold R. Eberle
President Worldcast Ministries and Publishing -Yakima, WA

"Mark Anderson has done a very thorough and excellent job with his new book, "Overcoming Roadblocks to Healing." Why is there such continual confusion and uncertainty concerning God's will for healing? Is healing the will of God for everyone? If healing is God's will, shouldn't it just take place automatically? Are there variables that can affect the will of God from coming to pass in your life?

*These and many more questions are answered from the Scriptures in **Overcoming Roadblocks to Healing**. Take time to read it through carefully with your Bible close by; you will discover and become confident that healing is for you!"*

-Steve C. Shank - www.SteveCShank.com
Boulder, CO - Pastor, Teacher, and Author of *Schizophrenic God? Finding Reality in Conflict, Confusion, and Contradiction*

"Some books are written from the lofty heights of academia, while others are written from the trenches of real life. This book is not

*based in theory, but on reality. Mark has lived between the ecstasy of seeing miracle healings, and the agony of those who were not healed. This book **Overcoming Road Blocks to Healing** will act as a personal guide to help you overcome the barriers to healing."*

-Pastor J.R. Polhemus - www.therock.org
Castle Rock, CO - Head pastor, The Rock

TABLE OF CONTENTS

ACKNOWLEDGEMENTS

Special thanks to my wife, Sharmila Anderson, who reviews all my writings, edits and makes sense out of all of them. Could not have done this without you, babe! It is fun watching Jesus show up and living this with you, all over the world!

To my father and mother, John and Jane Anderson. You were great examples to us kids of overcoming the hindrance to healing when mom had life-threatening cancer in 1974. We watched you learn the Word of God concerning healing, stand on the promises of God, resist the cancer and receive a miracle from Jesus. How you both live in health today, many years later. You are both a great inspiration!

To all of you, who I have watched in my lifetime who have stood despite the odds being against you. The Holy Spirit showed up and healed you. You are a great inspiration to many. A great example of our all-loving, powerful and resurrected Jesus, that He is the same yesterday, today and forever. Keep believing!

FOREWORD

Overcoming Roadblocks to Healing is an outstanding practical guide for those who are struggling to understand why healing does not come or last. At times, you may think the prayer of faith has failed or that you have done something to cause your sickness or pain to return. You may not know what to do next. I have been praying for the sick for many years. I have seen God do mighty things when praying for someone one time and then not see any results when praying for someone else another time. I have experienced victories and defeats in my own healing ministry and struggled at times with the mystery of why some do not get healed.

I believe Mark provides key insights from Scripture to help those who come against roadblocks in their healing. He not only offers strategy to get your healing, but gives personal experience where he has struggled to be healed or at times lost his healing. He tells you the truth about his struggle and the victory of overcoming his roadblocks to healing.

Mark exposes the lies that have caused believers to deny that healing exists or that it is not for today. He reveals the influence of Greek thought on our Western Christianity, which has caused a false belief that suffering and illness are the will of God for our lives. This misunderstanding has caused many to doubt that God can heal and their unwillingness to seek healing for their illness. Mark emphasizes that the truth of God's Word is the standard for which we should put our faith in. He stresses the need for believers to renew their minds by aligning thoughts and beliefs with the Word of God.

I believe this book should be read by every believer, especially those who need healing. It is a tremendous resource for those who have not walked in the healing ministry, to be aware of roadblocks in people's lives to healing. Thank you, Mark, for providing such a wonderful book that will help the church understand how to overcome the roadblocks to healing.

Randy Clark
Apostolic Network of Global Awakening
January 1, 2012

CHAPTER 1

ROADBLOCKS TO HEALING

The title of this book comes from a dream I had recently. I was driving a truck to a certain destination and I suddenly came to a roadblock. It looked like I would not be able to make it to my destination. As I approached the roadblock, I slowed down and saw a way around the roadblock. Then the dream ended. It was 3:30 a.m. and I thought nothing about this dream. I tried to fall back asleep, but could not and ended up getting up and praying for someone I knew who was struggling with cancer. Then the Lord showed me that this dream was meant to shed light on how to get around roadblocks when it comes to healing. Sad to say this person passed away; the family could not comprehend Jesus paying the price for our healing in His atonement.

The purpose of this book is not to make a person feel condemned or overwhelmed by roadblocks, but to be aware of things that can hinder Christ's healing power. My goal is to share some insight on hindrances to healing and help you move beyond those roadblocks and overcome them. I want to encourage you with the truth that there are ways around the roadblocks to healing. You are to move forward and press in for what rightfully belongs to you as a believer in Jesus.

If we believers will seek out the truth about healing, healing and miracles will become a regular occurrence. If we desire to experience miracles and healings on a regular basis, we need to pursue and seek after the truths in God's Word in order to lay a foundation that cannot be shaken. We have to seek after these truths as though seeking after hidden treasure. Christ's miracle working power is here. Do you want it?

NOT HUNGRY ENOUGH

Many see a roadblock to healing and think nothing can be done, when in fact that is not the final answer. *Jesus said, "Blessed are those who hunger and thirst for righteousness, For they shall be filled." (Matthew 5:6).* This is a principle Jesus established. We will be filled with what we hunger for. One roadblock that I often see when it comes to divine healing is a lack of hunger and thirsting. Many Christians do not like to venture outside the religious box they have put God in or have been raised to believe God is in when it comes to divine healing and miracles. There is no pressing in for it, but an attitude of whatever will be, will be. This attitude does not produce results and is damaging to the Kingdom of God.

In over 33 years of being in a healing ministry, I have watched people, hungry and thirsty to know more about the healing Jesus provided at Calvary and get filled with it: *Who Himself bore our sins in His own body on the tree, that we, having died to sins, might live for righteousness—by whose stripes you were healed (1 Peter 2:24).* They sought it out and found it and now have an unshakable foundation in God's Word for healings and miracles. They are living it and experiencing it! With healing it is not a matter of trying to get healed by God. His Word says we were already healed 2000 years ago (see Isaiah 53:3-5, Matthew 8:16-17 & 1 Peter 2:24). All we need to learn to do is tap into what was already provided for us by Jesus 2,000 years ago. We are healed because of what Jesus accomplished at Calvary.

Many believe that if healing does not occur immediately, then maybe it is not God's will to heal. In reality it is God's will to heal, but there may be roadblocks or hindrances that stand in the way of a person's complete healing. On the other hand, the absence of the physical manifestation of healing does not necessarily imply there are hindrances.

Let me explain. 1 Corinthians 12:9-10 talks about the gifts of healings (Greek- "of healing or remedy") and also the workings of miracles (Greek word *dunamis*- "miraculous ability, power for performing miracles"). Miracles can be instant healings or a supernatural change of event. God heals instantaneously (miracles) and supernaturally over a period of time (healings). Mark 16:18 says, *"they will lay hands on the sick, and they will recover,"* which implies some will be healed and recover over a period of time and some will be immediately healed.

Many have received prayer for physical healing, yet continue to suffer with an infirmity or disease that never seems to be healed. In this book, I will be unable to cover all the roadblocks or hindrances to healing. The purpose in this book is to search out and get rid of anything that may exist in your life that might hinder the miracle working power of Christ.

To successfully minister to the sick, it is advisable that all parties involved deal with attitudes in their lives that may hinder healing, thereby creating an environment that will be conducive to Christ's healing virtue! Too often, one does not have the time to deal with the hindrances before ministering healing. God in His infinite mercy and compassion has healed and will continue to heal people despite hindrances or roadblocks in their lives that would ordinarily impede healing. We have witnessed this personally time and again.

Often there are people who attend our campaigns that still worship idols, or attend to mock the campaign; many have been instantly healed by Jesus. These miracles cause many to turn to Christ. I am certain that these individuals had character traits that could be deemed as hindrances in receiving healing, yet were healed by the mercy of God. We have also seen Christians who have had hindrances or roadblocks to healing in their life but God has healed them. It is very important to understand that healing and miracles take place by God's grace. One cannot work up a healing or a miracle. Knowing this should make it easier to press in beyond any roadblock for healing or miracles knowing it is God's will to heal. Plain and simple, Jesus paid the price for our healing when He went to Calvary.

God expects more out of mature believers, however, and we should not be living our lives by the exceptions. James 4:17 says, *"Therefore to him that knows to do good and does not do it, to him it is sin."* Hosea 4:6 says, *"My people are destroyed for lack of knowledge...".* As Christians we should know and understand God's Word, which is His will. If healing does not come forth, we need to examine our lives for any negative strongholds that could hinder healing. We need to deal with them or, if there is no open door for the enemy, just simply learn to stand for what rightfully belongs to us (Ephesians 6:10). We will share more on how to stand in Chapter 6.

Jesus showed us the true example of faith by dealing with the root in Mark 11:20. If we are to walk in divine health as God desires we do, then we need to deal with the root problems in our life, not just the surface issues to see lasting change. We will talk more about that in Chapter 4. III John 2 says, *"Beloved, I pray that you may prosper in all things and be in health, just as your soul prospers."* The word soul in the Greek means mind, heart, feelings, desires and affections. As this area of our life lines up with the knowledge of God's word and will, then we can walk in divine health and prosperity.

NEGLECTING THE PHYSICAL BODY

There are some very basic hindrances to healing, like smoking, drinking, drug use, gluttony, laziness, etc. It is written in Proverbs 23:21, *"for the drunkard, and the glutton will come to poverty, and drowsiness will cloth a man with rags."* Often Christians are of the opinion that they do not need to take care of their flesh. Consuming junk food, lack of exercise, irregular sleeping habits, etc. will cause the body to deteriorate and be more vulnerable to quick aging, sickness and disease.

1 Timothy 4:8 says, *"For bodily exercise profits* (Greek- benefits) *a little* (Greek- is short lived), *but godliness is profitable for all things…"* In my opinion, even if it profits a little it should be practiced. God expects us to take care of our natural or physical bodies, which will only last for this life time. 1 Corinthians 6:19 says, *"or do you not know that your body is the temple of the Holy Spirit who is in you, whom you have from God, and you are not your own?"* 1 Corinthians 3:16 reiterates that our bodies house the

Holy Spirit and hence we have the responsibility of taking care of the house by all necessary means.

God made everything good, including food. One simple rule to staying healthy is if God did not make it, don't eat it. For example, white sugar is man-made and studies show it is very damaging to our immune system. It is best to avoid it. God made alternatives, like honey.

Over the years I have seen and heard of ministers who have ignored the care of their physical bodies to their extreme detriment. Evangelist Jack Coe stands out as one such example. He had a tremendous healing ministry in the 1940s and 50s. At that time, he owned a large Gospel tent, which was always packed to capacity when used. He was extremely passionate for the Lord and there were numerous occasions when he would preach for weeks at a time, three times a day. He slept very little and ate most of his meals at 3 a.m. Unfortunately, he was also overweight. He was a man driven by pride to prove he was better than other ministers. Sadly, he passed away at the age of 38, in the prime of his life.

Another minister who greatly inspired me, a missionary to Mexico, passed away at the age of 58. He had the largest Evangelical churches in Mexico at one time and burned with a passion for the lost. A close friend of mine worked with him in Mexico. He advised him to watch his diet, eat more healthy foods and to take care of his body. Unfortunately his words fell on deaf ears. This missionary was overweight. One day while preaching he dropped dead.

I believe that both these men are prime examples of individuals who had a deep passion for the Lord and the lost but, while they were spiritually strong, neglected the physical and passed away pre-maturely. Both of them had so much more to offer and accomplish, but ignoring the physical took its toll on them.

NO SEED PLANTED

The first thing we need to recognize is that it is God's will to heal our body. Jesus said, *"I came down from Heaven not to do my own will but the will of Him who sent me." (John 6:38)* Acts 10:38 says, *"How God anointed Jesus of Nazareth with the Holy Ghost and Power who went about doing good, healing all that were oppressed of the devil for God was with Him."* Never once did Jesus turn anyone down that came to Him for healing. It was only recorded once that He did not heal people and could do no mighty works because of their unbelief (Matthew 13:58).

Christians ask me why their community or church is not experiencing Christ's miracles and healings. One reason many churches do not experience healings and miracles is because there is little or no teaching or emphasis put on it. Maybe they do not see the need for it. God will only give you what you hunger for; this is a spiritual principal. Jesus said *"Blessed are those who hunger and thirst for righteousness, For they will be filled"* (Matthew 5:6). Jesus burned with a passion for healing. He was moved with compassion on suffering multitudes and that is one reason He performed so many miracles. If we burn with passion for His power so we can help suffering people, it will cause us to press in and be filled with His power to set the sick and demonized free.

1 Peter 1:23 says, *"Having been born again, not of corruptible seed but incorruptible, through the word of God which lives and abides forever."* When it comes to receiving healing, we cannot expect to receive a harvest on something we never planted. In

over 30 years of healing ministry, I have noticed a lot of Christians never receive healing because they never plant the seed for it, which is the word of God (according to 1 Peter 1:23 and Mark 4:1-20). Hebrews 11:6 says, *"without faith it is impossible to please God..."* . *"Faith* (for healing or whatever you need) *comes by hearing and hearing by the Word of God"* (Romans 10:17). Teaching and training is essential if we desire miracles and healings on a consistent basis. Faith simply believes in what God says in His word (Mark 11:22-24, Matthew 21:21-22, Romans 4:17-21). Our faith for healing cannot be built if we are constantly around people who claim that they are sick for God's glory and teach that God does not want to heal some people. It is important for us to know what the Word says on healing, as often when we believe for a healing, persecution will arise for the Word sake (Mark 4:17). Satan will attack us with doubts, trying to convince us that healing is not for us.

NOT UNDERSTANDING HOW TO PRAY PROPERLY

If we pray for the sick with the phrase 'if it be thy will," at the end, we are praying in unbelief. What has been promised to us in the Word is His will for us and we do not have to pray 'if it be thy will." We pray "if it be thy will" if it is a prayer of consecration. When we pray for the sick we are instructed to pray the prayer of faith. James 5:15-16 *"Is anyone among you sick? Let him call for the elders of the church, and let them pray over him anointing him with oil in the name of the Lord. And the prayer of faith will save the sick, and the Lord will raise him up. And if he has committed any sin they will be forgiven."* It is not the prayer of consecration or the prayer of uncertainty that will raise him up. It is the prayer of faith! Jesus ministered to the sick and demonized with great authority and faith, never wondering if it was the Father's will or not.

What is faith? Mark 11:24 says, *"Therefore I say to you, whatever things you ask when you pray, believe that you receive them, and you will have them."* Faith is believing you have it or believing you shall receive it. Who are we believing or trusting in? God, our Heavenly Father!

Notice James 5:15, *"any sin they will be forgiven."* What does that mean? In some cases, the very thing or root problem hindering someone's healing can be sin. Repenting and receiving forgiveness can close the door on the enemy. That is how to deal with the root of the problem causing the illness or infirmity so lasting health can be their portion.

1 John 5:14-15 says *"... whatever we ask according to His will* (His Word) *He hears us and we know that if He hears us we shall have the petitions desired of Him."* In the Lord's Prayer it says, *"thy will be done on Earth as it is in Heaven."* (Matthew 6:10). Is anyone sick in heaven? No! Than why should we, as born again believers, tolerate sickness or infirmities when Satan attacks us with it? Heaven longs to come down and invade earth with God's supernatural miracle working power. John 10:10 says, *"the thief* (Satan) *does not come but for to steal, and to kill and to destroy. I* (Jesus) *have come that you may have life, and that they may have it more abundantly."*

People who believe or preach that healing is not always God's will rarely see a miracle because they are not willing to take that step of faith by believing God's Word. If I preach that it is not always God's will to save a sinner, how many people would get saved? Not many! How can people be healed if we tell them it might not be God's will to heal? We need to believe and pray in faith, believing that God will heal. That is what His Word instructs us to do.

UNBELIEF

"And when He came to the multitude, a man came to Him, kneeling down to Him and saying, Lord have mercy on my son, for he is an epileptic and suffers severely; for he often falls into the fire and often into the water. So I brought him to Your disciples, but they could not cure him. Then Jesus answered and said, 'O faithless and perverse generation, how long shall I be with you? How long shall I bear with you? Bring him here to me.' And Jesus rebuked the demon, and it came out of him; and the child was cured from that very hour. Then the disciples came to Jesus privately and said, 'why could we not cast it out?' So Jesus said to them, 'Because of your unbelief; for assuredly, I say to you, if you have faith as a mustard seed, you will say to this mountain, move from here to there, and it will move, and nothing will be impossible for you. However this kind does not go out except by prayer and fasting" (Matthew 17:14-21).

Matthew 17:14-15 describes the incident of a father approaching Jesus; his son, who was an epileptic and a deaf mute (Mark 9:17), needed a miracle. The disciples were unable to help the boy (Mark 9:16). It is interesting to note that the boy was not healed instantly. Today, many would throw in the towel, saying, "I guess healing the boy is not God's will." Jesus puts the blame not on God's unwillingness to heal, but on the disciples' faithlessness (Mark 9:17) and unbelief (Mark 9:20). Since this was a problem in Jesus' day, could this possibly be a reason many are not healed today? This father, who wanted to see his son well, humbles himself and admits that he had unbelief, asking Jesus to help him with his unbelief (Mark 9: 24). Jesus took this man where he was at with his faith and helped him get his miracle for his son.

One thing we glean from this incident is that faithlessness and unbelief restrained this boy's miracle. Jesus' frustration over His disciple's unbelief is apparent. He wants us to be people of faith. Jesus said in Luke 18:8, *"...Nevertheless, when the Son of Man comes, will He really find faith on the earth?"*

DEMONIC HINDRANCE TO HEALING

Notice how, in order for this boy to be healed, Jesus had to cast out a demon (quoting *Humility The Hidden Key to Walking in Signs and Wonders* published by Destiny Image Chapter 7, Page 160, 166-167). Many believers battle with physical and mental afflictions. Is Jesus big enough to deliver you and bring health to you? One of the main hindrances to healing is demon spirits! In Mark 16:17-18, Jesus mentions two ways to minister healing to individuals needing healing. The first appears in verse 17: *"These signs shall follow those who believe: in my name they shall cast out demons..."* while the other appears in verse 18: *"They will lay hands on the sick and they will recover."* It has been a privilege to watch Jesus heal many thousands of people in our evangelistic outreaches or just one on one. I have to say that at least seventy five percent of those healed were healed as a result of casting demons out of them.

Demon spirits cause many physical and mental health problems, especially when we yield to them. Not all infirmities or sickness is caused by demons, but much sickness, disease, and infirmities are. Many try to ignore the demonic realm, hoping their problem will go away. Paul said, *"Lest Satan should take advantage of us; for we are not ignorant of his* (demonic) *devices"* (2 Corinthians 2:11). Healing does not take place by ignoring the problem. Acts 10:38 says, *"how God anointed Jesus of Nazareth with the Holy Spirit and with power, who went about doing good and healing all who were oppressed by the devil, for God was with Him.*" Notice Jesus healed all (nobody was left out) but we need to address who was causing the physical or mental pain and deal with it properly, knowing who we are in Christ and how big, powerful and willing to heal He really is.

GIVING THE DEMONS AND DEVIL TOO MUCH AT-TENTION

In Matthew 12:24, Satan is referred to as Beelzebub. Beelzebub means lord of the flies and dung. If you seriously meditate on this, you will see how defeated he really is. Flies are nothing more than mere irritants. It's the same with demons! Jesus talks about casting out demons with the finger of God. Does it take much effort? No! There is not much to say about waste (dung)! It's not something I like to give much attention to. This is what Satan and his demons are equivalent to. Beelzebub has no power other than what we give or allow him and his demons. Satan and his demons were defeated 2,000 years ago. Colossians 2:15, talking about Jesus, says, *"Having disarmed principalities and powers, He made a public spectacle of them, triumphing over them in it."* 1 John 3:8 says, *"He who sins is of the devil, for the devil has sinned from the beginning. For this purpose the Son of God was manifested, that He might destroy the works of the devil."* That is why our focus needs to be Christ, not demons.

Unfortunately, Christians often talk about all their problems and how the devil is beating them up. Many times the devil, and their problems, get more glory and attention than Jesus Christ. On the other hand, some ignore the demonic realm because of fear. Ignoring demons will not cause the problem to disappear. We understand who we are in Christ and how defeated demons are. Isaiah 14:16 tells us how surprised many will be when they finally see Lucifer or Satan: *"those who see you will gaze at you, And consider you saying is this the man who made the earth tremble, who shook kingdoms?"* Some day we will see with our eyes just how weak and defeated he really is.

When your focus is more on the problems and demons, than they will get the better of you. If the focus is Jesus, then they do not stand a chance. More of Jesus and less of us also means less problems and less of the devil and demons. More of Jesus also means more heaven on earth and less hell on earth. This is one way to live victorious over sin.

LACK OF PRAYER AND FASTING

In Matthew 17, Jesus makes a statement about His disciple's inability to cast out a deaf, mute and epileptic demon from a boy. First, their unbelief stood in the way (vs. 20), and then in verse 21 Jesus says, *"However, this kind does not go out except by prayer and fasting."* Fasting and prayer is not an option for mature believers and ministry leaders. There are many ways to fast. Daniel abstained from pleasant foods, meat and wine for 21 days (Daniel 10:3). We may fast by skipping meals or abstaining from television, but Biblical fasting always implies abstaining from food in some way. The main focus in this passage of scripture is to couple fasting with prayer.

When it came to prayer and fasting, Jesus did not tell people He had to go pray and fast to see a miracle. Fasting and prayer is not just for when a hard case comes our way, but a lifestyle. By having a lifestyle of prayer and fasting we are prepared for whatever may come our way.

Jesus states in Matthew 6:16, *"when you fast"* -not if you fast. Isaiah 58:6 says, *"Is this not the fast I have chosen: To loose the bonds of wickedness, to undo heavy burdens, to let the oppressed go free, and that you break every yoke?"* Fasting and prayer helps set the spiritual atmosphere for miracles and for freedom in people's lives. Isaiah 58:8 says when you fast, *"your healing shall spring forth speedily."* Fasting done correctly will even flush toxins out of our bodies. Fasting works to spiritually and physically cleanse us and to produce spiritual, physical health and bring spiritual breakthrough.

UNBELIEF, OFFENSE AND THE CRITICAL SPIRIT WORK TOGETHER

> *"Is this not the fast that I have chosen: to loose the bonds of wickedness, to undo the heavy burdens, to let the oppressed go free, and that you break every yoke? Is it not to share your bread with the hungry, and that you bring to your house the poor who are cast out; when you see the naked, that you cover him, and not hide yourself from your own flesh? Then your light shall break forth like the morning, Your healing shall spring forth speedily, and your righteousness shall go before you; the glory of the Lord shall be your rear guard. Then you shall call, and the Lord will answer; You shall cry and He will say, 'Here I am' if you take away the yoke from your midst, the pointing of the finger and speaking of wickedness."* (Isaiah 58:6-9)

Those ministering to the sick must note the importance of prayer and fasting in helping bring about a miracle intervention. Verse 6 refers to the freedom that everyone can experience when we set the spiritual atmosphere through prayer and fasting. Years ago I wish I had known what Isaiah 58 was all about. I would have cleansed myself and repented of character flaws that kept the miracles from flowing freely. Isaiah 58:6 says that prayer and fasting can *"break every yoke"*. What exactly is the yoke that God is talking about? Notice verse 9, *"Then you shall call, and the Lord will answer; you shall cry and He will say, Here I am if you take away the yoke from your midst, the pointing of the finger and speaking of wickedness."*

If we are critical and judgmental towards people and say negative things about any person, then we are pointing the finger and speaking wickedness. It can keep God from showing up in our midst and keep us from hearing His voice.

I have been in churches where people were critical of the preacher and had the attitude "okay, let's see what he can do." As a result, God did not move, and only a few sick people were healed. A judging or critical spirit can bring with it offense and unbelief. It can be to the extent that we terminate the life flow of God coming forth from people who God brought into our midst. These could be people God ordained to take us to another level spiritually or had a miracle for us from heaven. Jesus had the same problem in His day. I have witnessed this destructive power in people's lives.

In Mark 6:1-6, Jesus had come to bring God's miracle working power in their midst. However, instead of receiving their miracle from Jesus, they were offended by Him. Verse 5 points out the results; Jesus, the anointed one, could only heal a few sick people. Verse 6 says *"And He marveled because of their unbelief."*

In Luke 5:17-26, Jesus was able to heal one paralytic, yet the power of God was present to heal 'them' (Luke 5:17). Them means more than one! Their attitude kept the others and themselves from receiving from Jesus. Notice, unbelief (lack of faith) did not just come because they had no faith in Jesus, but it came because of offense, because of reasoning and a critical spirit in their midst as well (Luke 5:21).

Once, while I was ministering in North India, two people, Anil and Sanobai, had been blind, were healed and came forward to testify and demonstrate their miracle. It looked like the meetings were off to a great start. Another young lady, Rekha, had been crippled all her life with polio and was unable to walk. Later in the campaign, after prayer, she raised her crutches above her head and walked right up to the stage. My father-in-law, Major David Frank, had suffered a stroke that left him partially paralyzed. He also was partially deaf from injuries suffered during the war. He was completely healed during the campaign. In fact, prior to the campaign, he had confessed that he was going to be healed there. The power of God was present to heal many.

As the meetings continued, it seemed like the anointing for miracles dissipated. I could not understand why. Most of the time when our meetings started off powerfully like that, they continued to grow with intensity. The Lord showed me what had happened. The first night I had set my Bible down on the stage, as there was not much room. In the process, my foot accidentally brushed against the Bible. I did not even know I had done it. Later I heard that a couple of pastors were offended that I would do such a thing. The same pastors became very upset that I invited my wife to sit on the platform with me.

Later on in the conference, my wife laid hands on her sister, who was visiting, for the Baptism of the Holy Spirit. She was filled with the Holy Spirit and began speaking in tongues. The same pastors were very upset that she laid hands on her sister. At the conference, I was sharing that we as ministers should follow Jesus' example and serve others. After the teaching, these pastors took me off to the side and asked me how I could share such a teaching. They said, "people should be serving us, not us serving them." Even though I had worked with these pastors many times before, they were so offended over these issues that they no longer wanted to work with us.

Since that time, the Lord has shown me how offense can literally short-circuit the power of God from flowing to those who desperately need a miracle, as was true in this case. As we see in Mark 6, Jesus could only heal a few sick folk because of unbelief and offense. Unbelief and offense can stifle the corporate anointing for healing, but it can not stop the personal anointing God puts on someone's life for healing.

LACK OF LOVE AND COMPASSION

We have seen much legalism and apathy amongst ministers in places we have labored when it comes to serving and ministry to the lost and hurting. Jesus said the love of many would wax cold in these last days (Matthew 24:12). We need to guard our hearts against apathy. This attitude can greatly hinder healing. Jesus, miracles, signs and wonders take place in an atmosphere of compassion (Mark 1:40-45 & Matthew 14).

Another thing to be aware of when it comes to receiving healing from Jesus is to have a revelation of His love and compassion for you. Are you secure in His love for you? Self condemnation and guilt can greatly hinder healing to one's physical body: *"There is therefore now no condemnation to those who are in Christ Jesus, who do not walk according to the flesh, but according to the Spirit. For the law of the Spirit of life in Christ Jesus has made me free from the law of sin and death"* (Romans 8:1-2). There is no condemnation when we are in Christ and pursuing Him. Regarding the depth of Christ's love for each of us look at Ephesians 3:17-19. It says, *"Christ may dwell in your hearts through faith; that you, being rooted and grounded in love, may be able to comprehend with all the saints what is the width and length and depth and height to know the love of Christ which passes knowledge; that you may be filled with all the fullness of God."* Jesus is still moved with compassion towards you even as He was during the times He walked this earth in flesh and blood.

CHAPTER 2

THE NEGATIVE INFLUENCE OF GREEK PHILOSOPHY ON WESTERN CHRISTIANITY

The western Christian mindset has much of it's origin in Greek philosophy. People often ask Sharmila and I why all the miracles we witness are overseas when their churches do not see the same in North America. First, I tell them I do not agree. What these people are actually saying is that God cares more for the sick overseas than for the sick in North America. Look at Acts 10:34, *"...in truth I've perceived that God shows no partiality."* Romans 2:11 says, *"For there is no partiality with God."* God is no respecter of persons. If He heals people in India and Africa then He is willing and able to heal people in North America as well.

When praying for sickness or infirmities in Montana and Wyoming, we have seen many wonderful miracles, such as the crippled getting out of wheelchairs. On occasion we have had such powerful meetings in the USA that a larger percentage of people have been healed than in some of our most powerful campaigns overseas. It has a lot to do with their mindset and heart attitude towards healings and miracles.

Part of the reason so many Christians in the west struggle with divine healings and miracles is because of the influence of Greek philosophy and gnosticism. One example was Augustine, a great man of God, who had a major influence in the Roman Catholic Church and European government during the Middle Ages. He was greatly influenced by Greek philosophy before coming to Christ and mingled Greek philosophy with his understanding of the Scriptures. He was trained in Neoplatonism, which was a reworking of Platos ideas. His teachings greatly influenced other leaders, such as Martin Luther (Lutheran Church) and John Calvin (Calvinism). These three great men alone have greatly influenced western Christianity as we know it. They brought much good to Christianity, but at the same time took Christianity off the course of the ancient Hebrew and early Christian worldview in some areas.[1]

THE NATURAL/ SPIRITUAL DIVISION

Now let me explain how much of Christianity was influenced by Greek philosophy, asceticism, and gnosticism. Some of it has been passed right down to present day Christianity and our western way of thinking. Much of this mindset has become men's traditions *"making the Word of God of no effect"* (Mark 7:13). It

[1] *Christianity Unshackled, published by Destiny Image and written by Harold R. Eberle, is an excellent book. In this book, Harold takes you from the days of the early church right to present day Christianity and shows how the west has been deeply influenced by Greek philosophy, some of which is good and some of which I believe becomes a major roadblock to divine healing, miracles and much more. You can order Christianity Unshackled from our website: www.markandersonministries.com/ store. I highly recommend this book if you want to understand the historical side of our western Christianity and its influence in society. I am greatly indebted to Harold for writing this book and helping me to understand these things. Some of what I share below has come from the influence his book has had on me.*

influences our Christian belief system and is contrary to the way the ancient Jews and early Christians perceived things. This way of thinking has much deeper roots than many could ever imagine and it has affected the Body of Christ and nations in a very detrimental way. Many do not even realize that this disposition hinders the move of God.

The Greek philosopher Plato taught that there was a distinct separation between the spirit world and the physical world. Most Jews during biblical times did not believe this. In fact, there is no separation between the spiritual and physical realm. Cultures not influenced by Plato's philosophy have a much easier time receiving miracles and healings from Jesus because to them there is no separation between the spiritual and physical world. They do not reason away that God could do a miracle. After all, He is God the Creator. Nothing is impossible for Him. Some of the most powerful, undeniable miracles we see in our ministry are among Asians and Africans. Many of whom are from a Hindu or Muslim background. They do not know a whole lot about Jesus or Plato and Greek philosophy. It is easy for them to receive healings and miracles from God because they are more in tune to the spiritual and natural realm as one. They do not separate the physical and spiritual realm or the invisible and visible realms.

THE PROPER BALANCE

2 Timothy 1:7 says, *"For God has not given us a spirit of fear, but of power and of love and of a sound mind."* Sound mind in the Greek refers to a well balanced mind. Christianity through seeing many extremes was meant to be well balanced spiritually, mentally, physically and without compromise. To bring balance to this, the Bereans were people who believed the scriptures. One good thing we have learned from Greek philosophy is to study, ask questions and reason.

Acts 17:10-12 says, *"Then the brethren immediately sent Paul and Silas away by night to Berea. When they arrived, they went into the synagogue of the Jews. These were more fair-minded than those in Thessalonica, in that they received the word with all readiness, and searched the Scriptures daily to find out whether these things were so. Therefore many of them believed, and also not a few of the Greeks, prominent women as well as men."* The Greeks believed in testing things and proving something if they were so. 1 Thessalonians 5:21 says, *"Test all things; hold fast what is good."* That is what I have done with God's Word. His Word is proven, tested and it works. Once these Greeks saw something in the Word, they believed and acted on it.

This is where we need to draw the line; do not let your natural mind reason out what God can do. He is supernatural and moves beyond natural laws, longing for us to depend on Him and believe that He will move supernaturally on our behalf. Smith Wigglesworth had one of the most powerful healing ministries of the 20th century. He had a saying; "If God said it, I believe it, that settles it." If it is in God's Word believe it and act on it. Quit trying to reason it out. That was one reason the religious leaders of Jesus' days had a hard time receiving from Him; they reasoned things out too much (Luke 5:21).

Much of western Christianity is into reasoning things out with their mind and drawing a line - like Plato, Aristotle, Augustine and Calvin between the spiritual and natural or invisible and visible realms. It breeds unbelieving Christians who say they trust God and seem to be very spiritual, but only believe for things that can be worked up in the natural realm. Many times scriptures are taken out of context to support their beliefs. There is little or no dependence upon the supernatural healing or delivering power of Christ, who is the same yesterday, today and forever (Hebrews 13:8). Many even believe in salvation by grace or forgiveness, because it is something invisible like the wind, but when it comes to seeing a miraculous healing or deliverance from a demon in this physical realm, there is little or no faith for it. It is easier for them to have the cop out that it must not be God's will than to stand in faith for a miracle.

1 Thessolonians 5:23 says, *"Now may the God of peace Himself sanctify* (Greek- set apart) *you completely; and may your whole spirit, soul, and body be preserved blameless at the coming of our Lord Jesus Christ."* God made us a three part being; spirit, soul and body. We are to be balanced in all three areas. One way to do that is not to separate the spiritual and physical realms, but know both are completely integrated and work together.

WHEN AND WHERE DID THINGS CHANGE IN CHRISTIANITY?

During the Middle Ages, some church leaders took oaths of poverty and chastity because they believed and still believe today that they had to separate the spiritual from the physical world. Some believed in asceticism (physical suffering) or a form of gnosticism that said if it felt good it could not be of God. That is the reason behind oaths of poverty, chastity (permanent abstinence from sex) and asceticism (a belief in physical suffering).

During the enlightenment era other gnostics or agnostics began primarily focusing on the physical world because they were turned off by 'the Church or spiritual gnostics' who had focused only on the spiritual realm and basically said they were the ultimate truth and not to be questioned. They believed that God was far away and that man could never get close to Him, or that He did not exist, hence they should just go ahead eat, drink and be merry. If it feels good, do it!

Neither thought was balanced. God is a God of balance, both spiritually and naturally. In creation, God made it all good - spiritually and naturally or invisible and visible. For the early church and ancient Jews there was no separation of the spirit and physical realms. Work, worship and even sexual relations between a husband and wife were both spiritual and physical, and were good. The early Jews were not like the Greeks, who believed that only the spiritual was good. Notice that influence in our Western Christianity! Many times, as Christians who want to please God, we draw a line and think only the spiritual is good. If we are not focused on the spiritual we get easily condemned. That is not true with God!

Thomas Jefferson was a Christian who was mostly in tune with mental reason and the physical realm. He was greatly influenced by Christ, as well as enlightenment thought. Even believing in God, he greatly divided the natural and spiritual realm. He rewrote the New Testament, taking out all the miraculous things out like the virgin birth and the resurrection of Jesus; he entitled the book *The Life and Morals of Jesus of Nazareth*. I believe he loved Christ, but reduced the Bible to a book of morals because of the influence of enlightenment thought and Greek philosophy.

EXAMINATION OF MIDDLE AGES CHURCH VOWS

Let's briefly examine the vows these Middle Ages church leaders took because of separating the spiritual and natural realms. The first was vows of poverty, which they took because they might actually be able to enjoy life if they prospered. They believed the poorer you were, the more humble you could be.

To them, prosperity was something of the physical realm. They believed that you could only draw nearer to God by being poor.

Proverbs 22:4 says, *"By humility and the fear of the Lord are riches and honor and life."* Humility either attracts poverty (religious church tradition) or it attracts wealth (Biblical view/ 1 Timothy 6:17). *"...Let the LORD be magnified, Who has pleasure in the prosperity of His servant"* (Psalms 35:27). Will you choose religious tradition or the Bible as your source of truth? True Biblical humility attracts wealth and honor.

The next was vows of chastity. Augustine classified sex as something physical which could actually bring physical enjoyment. To be more spiritual, he felt a person needed to abstain from sex altogether. He believed the way sin was passed on to a baby or child was through sexual passions. Before coming to Christ, Augustine was promiscuous and after turning to Christ he still had battles with his sexual desires. He saw sexual desires as the strongest, most corrupt desires.

Some thoughts he had on sex were right and some he had were way off. Where is the balance, when you do not separate the spiritual and physical? Sex outside of marriage is sin and can bring many problems, such as the transferring of evil spirits, corrupt desires, ungodly soul ties, emotional problems, divorce, broken families, sexual disease, guilt, curses and much more. Augustine was right on his views of sex outside of marriage.

Sex within marriage can bring blessing, enjoyment, erotic pleasure, spiritual power can be released and so much more. It can supernaturally cause a man and woman to become one spirit, soul and body. Sex inside of marriage is both good naturally and spiritually; that is the way God ordained it. Contrary to Augustine, sex in marriage is not the way to pass sin on to our children. God blessed Adam and Eve and told them to be fruitful and multiply the earth (Genesis 1:28). Why would God tell them to commit something sinful if sex was evil, like Augustine believed? Augustine was way off on his views of sex and marriage.

Some church leaders in the Middle Ages felt they needed to suffer physically in order to subdue physical desires and thereby help them be more spiritual. This practice was called asceticism. This is where we get the belief that Christians were to suffer with sickness and disease to glorify Jesus and where the distortion came about regarding Paul's Thorn is the Flesh being sickness. I deal with the unscriptural misconceptions of Paul's Thorn in the Flesh in Chapter 5 of this book.

Job was the earliest book written in the Bible; 155 years before Moses! Job said, "...*The LORD gave, and the LORD has taken away; Blessed be the name of the LORD*" (Job 1:21). From many statements Job makes, God is into doing both good and evil at the same time. Steve C. Shank in his excellent book *Schizophrenic God? Finding Reality in Conflict, Confusion, and Contradiction* has a whole chapter on Job's theology and how God had to correct Him. Job never once refers to Satan, the devil or demons, and accused God of their things, not knowing any better. Many Calvinists glean many beliefs from Job's erroneous theology. God had to correct his incorrect theology. God said to Job, "*To justify yourself, will you condemn Me?*" (Job 40:8, Moffatt). Though Job's theology was off and he did not understand many things, his heart remained right before God and He was blessed with twice as much in the end (Job 42:10).

It is pretty sad when we have Jesus as our standard, yet many build their doctrines and beliefs on what Job said or what religious tradition teaches, rather than the Word of God. I ministered on the streets of Ullan Bator, Mongolia in 1992, right after communism fell in Mongolia. There were only 1,000 Christians in the country at that time. We saw many undeniable healings and miracles and close to 300 salvations on the streets of Ullan Bator. We ran into resistance from the only pastor in the country. He was greatly entrenched in Calvinism and knew a lot scripture and did not believe the book of Acts was for today. He was a Wycliffe Bible Translator who was translating the Bible into the native tongue. The first book he translated for the Mongols was the book of Job. The book of Job was the foundation he laid for the early believers in Mongolia in those days. We wonder why so many churches struggle in these countries; importing a western form of Christianity instead of Jesus is not the answer.

WAS JESUS OR THE BIBLE INTO A NATURAL/SPIRITUAL DIVISION?

Let's take a look at what Jesus and the Bible have to say about the natural/spiritual division. We will see clearly through the scriptures that the ancient Jews and Jesus did not divide these two realms, but operated with both the spiritual and natural or invisible and visible realms being fully integrated or as one. This is important to understand if you want to see heaven invade this earth with Christ's miracles, healings, signs and wonders.

First off, I want to say I believe Jesus is perfect theology. You can't have better theology than what He taught. In John 14:9, *"Jesus said to him, "Have I been with you so long, and yet you have not known Me, Philip? He who has seen Me has seen the Father; so how can you say, 'Show us the Father'?"* He also said in John 6:38, *"For I have come down from heaven, not to do My own will, but the will of Him who sent Me."* Hebrews 1:3 says, *"who being the brightness of His glory and the express image of His person, and upholding all things by the word of His power..."* John 1:14 says, *"And the Word became flesh and dwelt among us..."* I do not think you can get better theology than Jesus, the Living Word made manifest. As followers of Christ, we need to filter all our theology through Jesus and what He accomplished at Calvary. It is important as believers to live our lives on the right side of the cross. Many Christians live their life as if Jesus never went to the cross. We are living under a New Covenant, which is much better than any previous covenant because Jesus laid down His life and was raised from the dead.

Let's look at Jesus' worldview. He said in Matthew 16:19, *"And I will give you the keys of the kingdom of heaven, and whatever you bind* (Greek- forbid) *on earth will be bound in heaven, and whatever you loose* (Greek- allow) *on earth will be loosed in heaven."* Notice Jesus said that He will give us the keys to the greatest Kingdom in the Universe. The Kingdom of Heaven! To understand this better, let me quote from my book *You Can Tap Into Christ's Healing Power*:

> *Matthew 16:19, is based on the Greek concept of mirror imaging. This implies affecting the spiritual realm for success in the physical realm. Everything that happens in the physical realm, such as miracles or a move of the Holy Spirit came as a result of affecting the spiritual realm first. We need to affect the spiritual realm to see results in the physical realm. The Israelites understood this concept and were in tune to the spiritual realm. They knew that if they could affect the spiritual realm they would see great success in the physical realm. They thus called upon the living God with fasting and prayer to affect the spiritual and the natural realm as King Jehoshaphat did when the combined*

armies of Moab, Ammon and others besieged Judah and there appeared no way out for Judah (2 Chronicles 20:1-30). *They were greatly outnumbered!*

After praying, fasting and affecting the spiritual realm God spoke through a prophet. 2 Chronicles 20:15, "And he (the prophet Jahaziel) said, Listen, all you of Judah and you inhabitants of Jerusalem, and you, King Jehoshaphat! Thus says the Lord to you: Do not be afraid nor dismayed because of this great multitude, for the battle is not yours, but God's." King Jehoshaphat understood that God was going to deliver Judah from the vast enemy army and instead of sending soldiers out to face the enemy, he sent the praise and worship teams to worship God before the enemy. As they were praising God, the Lord sent ambushments against the enemy, and the enemy was defeated.

In Isaiah 37:36, the Lord sent one angel who killed 185,000 Assyrians, once again protecting Judah from the enemy. King Hezekiah prayed to the Lord, affecting the spiritual realm, and saw the results in the physical realm. Many nominal Christians think angels are just fat little naked babies as portrayed on their glass stained windows. I guarantee you a fat little naked baby could not kill 185,000 people. Angels are powerful. Hebrews 1:14 says, "Are they not all ministering spirits sent forth to minister for those who will inherit salvation?" Angels move on our behalf when we affect the spiritual realm.

Jesus said in Luke 12:8-9 "Also I say unto you, whoever confesses Me before men, Him the Son of Man will confess before the angels of God. But He who denies Me before men will be denied before the angels of God." When we are confessing Christ before men we are setting a spiritual force into motion. God's angels are going out to minister to the heirs of Salvation.

The Babylonians understood and acted upon this principle of mirror imaging as well. The difference lay in the fact that they called upon evil powers for victory. They built a city and buried it underground. Then they built the replica of that city above the ground in order to call upon the powers of the underworld. They affected the spiritual realm and as a result won great battles and conquered many in their time.[2]

What we are basically doing according to this principal of mirror imagining in Matthew 16:19 is reflecting heaven onto the earth by not separating the spiritual and natural or invisible and visible realms. With the keys Jesus gave us, we can use our authority in the physical realm to affect the spiritual realm and thus see the manifestation of that in this physical realm. So for Jesus there was no separating these two realms; they are both one and fully integrated. That is why Jesus prayed, *"Your kingdom come. Your will be done on earth* (physical realm) *as it is in heaven* (spiritual realm)."* (Matthew 6:10) We are to reflect God's Kingdom here on planet Earth. Why would Jesus pray your will be done if, like Augustine and Calvin believed, everything good and bad that happens in life is God's will? It is clear there are many things happening on this earth that are not God's will. That is why Jesus came to do the will of the Father (John 6:38) and destroy the works (will) of the devil (1 John 3:8).

Paul said, *"For we walk by faith, not by sight"* (2 Corinthians 5:7). Many in Christian circles are doing everything they can in the natural or physical realm to bring about the answers to their prayers. Their faith is totally dependent on what can be worked up in the natural realm, what they feel, see, hear, etc. Faith in God moves beyond the physical realm or what can be worked up

[2] *Chapter 6, You Can Tap Into Christ's Healing Power*

in the physical realm into affecting the spiritual realm and bringing the manifestation into the physical realm.

The Body of Christ as a whole has become very good at just
coping, being overcome and barely making it by because of the
influence of Greek philosophy in our western form of Christianity. Much of western Christianity is where the supernatural
has been removed and reduced to what can be worked up in
the natural realm because of the natural/spiritual division. Many
western-influenced Christians do not even realize they are more
influenced by Greek philosophy than by the Bible. Some Christians do not receive divine healing because they are only focused
on what comes naturally. Their mindset is such that they make it
hard for God to do anything supernatural in their lives. They lim-
it God to what can be done naturally, such as through medicine
or holistic practices only, not relying on the supernatural ability
of the Holy Spirit that is within us. Many Christians operate
from this perspective.

2 Timothy 3:5 talks about these churches or Christians in the
last days; it says, *"having a form of godliness but denying its power.
And from such people turn away!"* Those Christians who focus on
what can be done naturally also separate the natural and spiritual
realm by their attitude. We need to be in tune with both realms
and not separate the natural and spiritual realm. Unfortunately
because of the influence of Greek thought on the west, there is
often a priority for either the spiritual or physical. With God
there is no prioritizing of either. Healing and miracles flow much
easier in an environment where there is no separation of the spiritual and natural. Individuals have received healing breakthroughs
when they learned not to divide the natural and spiritual realm.

In the USA, there are a number of churches that we minister

in where we know God will move powerfully because the pastor and congregation prepare for a move of the Spirit. They know that God is not a respecter of persons. They simply believe and put a draw on the Holy Spirit that resides in us. They do not separate the physical and spiritual realm and believe God can invade the physical realm. The atmosphere is conducive for miracles. As a result, miracles and healings break out all over those churches. It really has little to do with us, but a lot to do with the mindset that believes nothing is impossible for Jesus and He can invade this physical realm.

Hebrews 11:1-3 says, *"Now faith is the substance of things hoped for, the evidence of things not seen. For by it the elders obtained a good testimony. By faith we understand that the worlds were framed by the word of God, so that the things which are seen were not made of things which are visible."* Faith is what can actually bring about something (physical) out of nothing (invisible). For more on faith, see Chapter 4. Faith activates the miracle working power of God the same way fear activates Satan's destructive power.

John 8:31-32 says, *"Then Jesus said to those Jews who believed Him, "If you abide* (Greek- continue) *in My word, you are My disciples indeed. And you shall know the truth, and the truth shall make you free."* It is one thing to know scriptures like many Christians do and quite another thing to continue in the Word, to know and experience the Word working in your life. Many Christians know the truth of God's Word but are still bound. Mental assent to the Word of God will not cut it. The Bible is spiritual truth. If someone is sick or diseased the fact is they are sick or diseased. This is not mind over matter or ignore it and it will go away. Jesus did not tell us to ignore the mountain but to face the mountain and speak to it in faith believing that it would be removed (Mark 11:22-23). Bill Johnson says, *"Faith doesn't deny a problem's existence. It denies it a place of influence.*" The mountain before you is the truth (fact) in the physical realm. Here is the difference with those who do not separate the two realms as Augustine and Calvin did. You can take spiritual truth (the Word of God) which supersedes physical facts and apply with faith and watch the spiritual truth do away with the physical facts (physical realm truth) by creating something (physical) out of nothing (invisible). That is how faith in God's Word works. A whole lot of fun!

BEING WELL BALANCED IN ALL AREAS OF YOUR LIFE

Quoted from *Humility The Hidden Key to Walking in Signs and Wonders* published by Destiny Image Chapter 4 Page 95-96.

While we are on this subject, another misconception because of Greek philosophy getting into western Christianity is the idea of just focusing on the spirit and neglecting the physical body. 1 Timothy 4:8 says, "For bodily exercise profits (Greek- benefits or blessings) a little, but godliness is profitable for all things, having promise of the life that now is and of that which is to come." Exercise does profit us a little (meaning temporarily for this lifetime). Does that mean we avoid it? A spiritual gnostic or someone who is "super-spiritual" might take that verse and say that we do not need to exercise or focus on the body. We only need the spiritual! Studies have shown that among Christians, obesity is more of a problem than among the non-religious. Obesity, of course, leads to many health problems. I believe this is because many Christians ignore the mental and physical realm and only concentrate on the spiritual. I have been there and done that, focusing only on the spiritual to the point I became so spiritually spaced out that I was not much earthly good. It made me very imbalanced and ineffective in areas of my life.

Not only does our family believe God for divine health, but we do our part to walk in health by eating right, fasting, taking vitamins, exercising, etc. We believe that is what God desires for us to do and it has paid off in keeping us healthy, energetic and active. Rarely has there been any sickness in our family. We believe in being well balanced in spirit, mind and body (1 Thessolonians 5:23).

We need to humble ourselves and repent if we are not taking care of the temple of the Holy Ghost that we are entrusted with (1 Corinthians 3:16-17). You will live much longer and accomplish much more for the Kingdom of God if you take care of yourself physically: Proverbs 23:20-21 says, "Do not mix with winebibbers, Or with gluttonous eaters of meat; For the drunkard and the glutton will come to poverty, And drowsiness will clothe a man with rags."

Sometimes Christians focus on the spiritual to the point they become physically lazy and are no earthly good. This often leads to health problems. We need to be balanced in spirit, soul and body. We are not called to run around only being spiritual, without time or energy to serve the least of these. If you are healthy you will live longer and be able to accomplish much more for the Kingdom of God.

IS GOD SCHIZOPHRENIC?

Steve C. Shank, author of *Schizophrenic God? Finding Reality in Conflict, Confusion, and Contradiction,* gives us some insight how to overcome the western mindset that has been greatly influenced by Greek philosophy. I am greatly indebted to him for his insight into both the good and the negative influences of Augustine, John Calvin and other early church leaders and what they brought into the western church. His book is by far the best book I have ever read on the subject of the Sovereignty of God, Calvinism and what the Bible and early church leaders had to say about it. In Steve Shank's words:

> *First, we start with the fact that Jesus is the Healer. We must go to the Gospels and carefully look at how He viewed sickness. Did He see it as a blessing in disguise that God the Father placed on people to help them grow spiritually? Did He ever tell a person, "You'll be better off incapacitated with this disease. You will learn in the long run that your terminal condition is really for your own good?" When we search the Scriptures, we can not find anything close to that in Jesus' practices or in His preaching. He viewed sickness and disease as an enemy to the human race and treated those who were sick as victims who needed to be healed and restored.*

> *When Jesus came on the scene He aggressively went about healing and destroying the works of the devil in people's lives ... For this purpose the Son of God was manifested, that He might destroy the works of the devil (1 John 3:8). He trained and commissioned the twelve-giving them power and authority to heal ALL diseases (see Luke 9:1). He trained and commissioned seventy-two others to heal the sick in all the towns and villages where He sent them (see Luke 10:1,9).*

> *Jesus and His swat team of eighty-four aggressively came against sickness wherever they went! Jesus clearly established, once and for all, that sickness is not a blessing but a curse that needs to be removed from the human race.*

> *Some people mistakenly think that healing ended in Bible days and God does not intend for people to be healed today. Let's pay*

close attention to Jesus and let Him settle the issue. In Matthew 28:16-20, Jesus commissions the eleven and tells them to make disciples in all the nations, teaching them to observe everything that He had already taught them. In other words, continually perpetuate the same Gospel that He taught, practiced, and demonstrated to them. Jesus' Gospel most certainly included healing. We have no other picture or pattern of the Gospel than the one that Jesus taught, practiced in Matthew, Mark, Luke, and John. A large part of Jesus' Gospel was healing.

Jesus came to show us God's heart and will for people. Jesus is the visible representation of the unseen God. He is the image of the invisible God, the firstborn over all creation (see Colossians 1:15). Every act of healing clearly portrayed that Father God wants people healed and set free! Jesus is the will of God made flesh-made visible for all of us to see. He takes all the mystery and uncertainty out of the question, "Does God really want to heal me?" Of course He does!

Faith begins where the will of God is known and Jesus makes it clear and eliminates all uncertainty - healing is God's will for all people, for all time.

One roadblock I want to examine is a very subtle one. It dates back to around 400AD, so it is very inbred and established in the western church mindset. It was taught by early church father Augustine, and became the established worldview of the church at that time. What Augustine taught was that everything that happens in a person's life is the direct will of God. We should not even attribute what appears to be evil to the will of demons or wicked people, but consider all things to be the direct will of God. This viewpoint was taught to Christians for hundreds and hundreds of years and is still believed by a surprising number of people today. You may have never heard of Augustine and yet still have bits and pieces of his mindset in your belief system. When calamity, sickness, or disease hit, many people will say things like this, "Why God? What have I done to deserve this from You?" or "God has some kind of reason behind this or it never would have happened!" or "You know that the ways of God are mysterious and past finding out."

All of this type of reasoning leaves out a major factor - we have an enemy, an adversary, who is continually looking for an opportunity to devour and destroy us! Be sober, be vigilant; because your adversary the devil walks about like a roaring lion, seeking whom he may devour. Resist him, steadfast in the faith ... (1 Peter 5:8-9). ...Nor give place to the devil (Ephesians 4:27). Therefore take up the whole armor of God, that you may be able to withstand in the evil day, and having done all, to stand. Stand therefore... (Ephesians 6:13-14). Augustine disagreed with that Bible viewpoint and instead taught that all things, even evil things, come directly from God and therefore are the will of God.[3]

I want to add something to what Steve Shank has said in that last sentence. Augustine's (as well as John Calvin's) worldview was contrary to the Bible and many early church leaders. They have reduced Christianity to some of the same beliefs as Islam

---

[3] *For an in-depth study of this extreme sovereignty viewpoint and other perplexing questions about God's will, get Steve C. Shank's book: Schizophrenic God? Finding Reality in Conflict, Confusion, and Contradiction, published by Destiny Image, www.SteveCShank.com. You can order Schizophrenic God? Finding Reality in Conflict, Confusion, and Contradiction from our website www.markandersonministries.com/store. I highly recommend it*

and Hinduism. The Muslims believe that whatever happens in this life, good or bad, is Allah's (God the Creator to Muslim people) will for the person. The Muslim concept of who and what God the Creator is like is not similar to what I hold to be true. Hindus believe that whatever good or bad happens in this life is the will of the Hindu gods (demons) and this is your karma in life. Karma is the Hindu's version of sowing and reaping, there is no grace involved. That is one belief proposed by Augustine and John Calvin, Steve and I strongly disagree with.

Those who believe that God is behind both good and bad occurrences say everything good or bad (evil) works together for the good of all people in this world. One place they get this is from taking Romans 8:28 out of context; which says, *"and we know that all things work together for good to those who love God, to those who are the called according to His purpose."* Do all things good and bad automatically work together for good, like Augustine and Calvin believed? It is very important not to pull things out of context to make it fit our beliefs. I do not believe all things necessarily work for the good of every person on this planet. Notice how that verse starts, with an 'and'. That means there is something tied to that verse before that. Look at Romans 8:26-27 just before verse 28: *"Likewise the Spirit also helps in our weaknesses. For we do not know what we should pray for as we ought, but the Spirit Himself makes intercession for us with groanings which cannot be uttered* (Greek says groanings, which can't be uttered in articulate speech or known speech). *Now He who searches the hearts knows what the mind of the Spirit is, because He makes intercession for the saints according to the will of God."*

Notice the prior verses are talking about the Holy Spirit interceding through us "according to the will of God." He does this when we are praying in the Spirit or tongues, just like Jesus prayed before raising Lazarus from the dead (1 Corinthians 14: 13-15, 18, John 11: 33 & 38). Praying like this is what helps us flow in the power of the Holy Spirit especially in an environment where the miracles of Jesus are needed. My testimony of how I was called into ministry revolves around these verses. The purpose of praying in the Spirit is to allow the Holy Spirit to pray through us for God's will to be done. He, Jesus, makes intercession for us (Hebrews 7:25). The Holy Spirit helps pray through us according to His will by praying through us in the Spirit or tongues.

Notice what 1 John 5:14-15 says if we pray for something according to His will: *"Now this is the confidence that we have in Him, that if we ask anything according to His will, He hears us. And if we know that He hears us, whatever we ask, we know that we have the petitions that we have asked of Him."* If the Holy Spirit is praying through us for God's will to be done, don't you think all things will work together for your good? I have seen both good and bad things work together for my good when I have allowed the Holy Spirit to pray through me. There is no such thing as everything just automatically working together for the good of every person on this planet, contrary to Augustine and Calvin's belief and teachings. I could give you hundreds of stories of things not working together for the good of people in this world.

Notice in Romans 8:28: *"...all things work together for good to those who love God, to those who are the called according to His purpose."* Let's say, for example, as a Christian I am not fitting into the purpose and plan that God has for my life. Could things end up not working together for my good? I have seen Christians all over the world, not fitting into God's plan and purpose for their life — they end up living a miserable and defeated life. All things do not work together for good if we understand these verses and live in reality. All things can work together for the good if we are doing what Romans 8:26 - 28 says to do. Steve Shank continued:

Most people in North America and Western Europe believe that whatever is currently happening in their own physical/circumstantial realm is somehow God's will for their lives. "Well, it must be God's will for me or it wouldn't be happening!" they reason. So, they have actually placed their faith [when it comes to determining the will of God] in the material/physical realm; and when it comes to our subject of healing, they take a "seeing-is-believing" approach. "Go ahead and pray," they say, "and if all the symptoms leave my body, then I'll know it was God's will to heal me; and if there's no change in my body, then I'll know that it's not His will to heal me." Their faith is in what they can see and feel. They are entrenched in the Thomas syndrome and Jesus called that "faithless" (see John 20:24-29).

The physical realm is what we consider last and it is never where we place our faith. What is happening physically does not determine the will of God for healing or anything else. Faith's realm and function is always that of the unseen and unfelt; faith is the evidence of things NOT seen (see Hebrews 11:1). Faith is what you exercise in Jesus and His Word BEFORE you can see or feel your healing. Once your healing can be seen and felt, faith has served its purpose and performed its function.

CHAPTER 3

NOT DEPENDENT ON CHRIST THE HEALER

2 Chronicles 16:12-13 states: *"And in the thirty-ninth year of his reign, Asa became diseased in his feet and his malady was severe; yet in his disease he did not seek the Lord, but the physicians. So Asa rested with his fathers; he died in the forty-first year of his reign."*

King Hezekiah was informed by the prophet to set his house in order, as he was surely going to die. Hezekiah immediately sought the Lord, who had mercy on him, took away the death sentence and added fifteen more years to his life (Isaiah 38:1-5). King Asa, a godly king, sought the physicians rather than God, dying a short while after being afflicted by the foot disease.

Unfortunately, many Christians today will first put their dependence on doctors to obtain health and healing, not even looking to God. I am not against doctors or consulting doctors, but I feel it is wrong when, as believers in Jesus, our first response to sickness or infirmities is the doctor or the medicine cabinet, without even considering God and His Word. We know doctors for the most part work with God to help bring about health and healing. Doctors are not our source for divine health; Jesus is! Many have made doctors the source for their health rather than God and His Word. That is why most believers have learned to cope with sickness and infirmities rather than receive a healing from God. I find it ironic that many Christians will say healing is not for today or are not sure that God wants them healed, yet they will run to the doctors and do their best to gain healing through doctors or medicine. They won't even look to God or pray for healing, even though He shows us clearly in His word he longs to see us healed or heathly.

King Asa, despite being a godly king, died of a foot disease because he did not look to God, but to physicians involved with sorcery. The words witchcraft and sorcery found in Galatians 5:20 and Revelations 21:8 are similar. The Greek word is *pharmakeia*, where we get the word pharmacy, referring to drugs and medicines that change a person's behavior and gives temporary relief to suffering. Many people refuse to get to the 'root of their problems' and look for temporary remedies that do not last. In the long run it breeds or brings a person or society to a place of dependence on drugs, addiction or a state of coping rather than overcoming. Not everything with medicines and drugs is bad. There is a balance. Where is the balance found? In God's word and in this book!

During the first century, many would flock to priests of pagan or demonic religions to find relief from suffering. These priests would give them drugs mixed with wine to bring temporary relief. In order to feel good, people kept returning to the priests when the drug wore off. It brought people to place of addiction and dependency on that drug. This is what is referred to as witchcraft and sorcery in the New Testament. It can open a person up to the demonic realm where demons have a legal right to take the illness or infirmity to a whole new level.

It is a problem that plagues our society today with both Christians and non-Christians. The only difference it is much worse today and covered up. One reason is because of the Greek mindset that separates the spiritual and natural realms. If we could only see in the spirit realm, I guarantee we would not do many of things we do. God's word gives us insight into the spirit realm. Many today have become dependent on 'pharmakeia' (pharmacy) to keep them going. It is a booming business in our country. In most Christian circles, there is little or no looking to Christ and the healing and divine health He provides. Just pop a pill!

Many believers are addicted to pills to deal with depression. What happened to the fruit of joy that resides in every Born Again believer by the power of the Holy Spirit? (Galatians 5:22-23) There are many who, with the slightest bit of pain or belief in the anticipation of pain, pop pain pills often and regularly, not even concerned what the effect might be to their physical body or mind.

Many of our prisons and jails are loaded with people addicted to Ridalan. Rather than dealing with the root problem, we just give kids a pill. Many already know, most kids who are given Ridalan will end up in prison or jail. This is the fruit of not depending on Christ and His word for healing and health.

You do not have to go far. Just look at all the television commercials about drugs and lawsuits against certain drugs. "Take this pill. It will solve your problem, but beware it can have these 20 side effects. And of course if it almost kills you or makes you feel suicidal, please contact your doctor so he can prescribe a different drug." Thank God for the invention of DVRs to tune out all these commercials! The society we live in is a society addicted to pharmakeia. I know that not all drugs are bad. Look at the overall fruit of a people dependent on drugs to help them cope. A very unhealthy society! I know there is a fine line balance; I would highly recommend finding it!

Despite being healthy, active and running most of his life, my father slowed down a bit and was diagnosed with type II diabetes in his early 70's. Instead of just coping with diabetes or getting a quick fix with drugs and medicine, he did research on how to deal with his problem. Hosea 4:6 says, *"my people are destroyed for lack of knowledge."* With a bit of knowledge on diabetes and prayer, he decided to get back to regular exercise and watching his diet. Within a short time, he lost a little bit of weight and has been very healthy and free of diabetes for the past five years. Our family has made it a priority to trust God first and foremost, praying for healing. As a result, we have rarely needed medical intervention. We thank God for the medical assurance found in His Word. We have watched God heal instantly or supernaturally over time whenever we have prayed for healing. Proverbs 4:20-22: *"My son, give attention to my words; incline your ears to my sayings. Do not let them depart from your eyes; Keep them in the midst of your heart; For they are life to those who find them, and health* (Hebrew- medicine) *to all their flesh."* I have witnessed many Christians with complete dependence on God for healing, despite all the odds against them. I have watched God come through and heal their bodies, instantly or supernaturally over a period of time, as they continued to stand for their healing.

When the woman with the issue of blood had done everything with doctors to bring about her healing and health, the doctors gave her the bad news; there was no hope for her. She had spent all her money on the doctors and was not better, but grew worse. Most doctors are limited to this natural realm. Many are in need of something beyond what the natural realm can offer. When this same woman heard of Jesus' healing power and pressed to get her healing, she was completely healed. Mark 5:34 shows us, *"And He* (Jesus) *said to her, "Daughter, your faith has made you well. Go in peace, and be healed of your affliction."* Jesus desires that we press in and learn to walk in faith, just like this woman did.

I also know Christians who gave up believing because some Christian leaders told them that maybe it was not God's will to heal them. Unfortunately, they threw in the towel and stopped trusting God. They did everything in the natural realm to get better, but only got worse and even died.

ASHAMED OF THE GOSPEL OF CHRIST

What it ultimately comes down to is our beliefs. Romans 1:16: *"For I am not ashamed of the Gospel of Christ, for it is power of God to salvation for everyone who believes, for the Jew first and also for the Greek."* Whenever the Gospel of Christ is preached and received it is the "power of God unto salvation." The Greek word for salvation includes forgiveness, healing, deliverance, prosperity, protection and much more.

Jesus said in Luke 12:8-9, *"Also I say to you, whoever confesses Me before men, him the Son of Man also will confess before the angels of God. But he who denies Me before men will be denied before the angels of God."* It is very clear if we confess Jesus before men we set a spiritual force into motion and angels go out to work on our behalf (Psalms 103:20-21). Angels are released to come to our aid according to these verses. If we are ashamed of Jesus and

His Gospel or try not to rock the boat by speaking of Jesus, we are denied before the angels of God and the power of God unto salvation is not ours to experience.

NOT ALLOWING JESUS TO BE THE SAME YESTERDAY, TODAY AND FOREVER

Quoted from *Humility The Hidden Key to Walking in Signs and Wonders* published by Destiny Image, Chapter 7 Page 153-154:

Hebrews 13:8 says, "Jesus Christ is the same yesterday, today, and forever." Jesus has not changed. He is still the same today. John 6:2 says, "Then a great multitude followed Him, because they saw His signs which He performed on those who were diseased." Is Jesus still doing signs, wonders and miracles in your midst like He did in the Gospel accounts? If not, He has not changed but we could have changed in a way that is not allowing Him to be the same today. With humility, we need to recognize the problem is ours, not His.

A false humility has crept into the church that says, "I do not want to bother Christ for His miracles or healings. I just want to seek His face, not His hand." That statement may sound good, but is that really allowing Him to be the same yesterday, today and forever? I know for a fact that Jesus was whipped and beaten beyond recognition for us, so we could be healed.[4] He is not at all bothered by us asking or believing Him for miracles. He is not bothered by us asking for healing or provision, especially when it is for others we may be ministering to. He is a big God who wants to pour out His love on the poor, hurting, unloved and on you!

[4] *the Hebrew word is 'rapha' meaning physical healing; see Isaiah 53:3-5, Matthew 8:16-17 and 1 Peter 2:24*

DWELLING ON THE NEGATIVE

In John 5:1-16, Jesus healed a man who had been crippled for 38 years. He was the only one healed by the pool of Bethesda (House of Grace) among all the sick and crippled who were laid there. Also, in Luke 5:17 *"and the power of the Lord was present to heal them."* 'Them' always implies more than one. Yet only one crippled man was healed in Luke 5:17-26. As we read on, one can see that the religious leaders reasoned and were offended with Jesus (Luke 5:21). Could that have hindered Christ's miracle power?

When similar miracles occur today, you can be sure that the media and many Christians will zero in on those who were not healed or lost their healing, instead of rejoicing over the ones who were healed. Their focus is distorted! There were those in the gospel accounts who were not healed, but the gospel accounts zero in on those who received their healings more than ones who did not. When we get good at the Gospel (which means 'good news'), sharing the good news or testimonies of our great big God it becomes the seed that reproduces miracles time and time again.

Many Christians permit the media or negative circumstances to be the lens through which they perceive God. Later, when they require a healing or miracle from God, they wonder why they don't receive it. They have lost track of what God has done and focus on what He has not done. Some get offended with God or healing ministries because healing is not taking place the way they would like it to. Proverbs 23:7 says, *"as a man thinks in his heart so is he."* Jesus said, *"For out of the abundance of the heart the mouth speaks"* (Matthew 12:34). You become what you dwell on and what you focus on. Soon you begin speaking it out. Do you want to know your future? Just listen to what comes out of your mouth. That is your future. If you do not like what you are hearing, seeing and experiencing, than it is time to change your focus and what you are pumping into your mind and heart. Whatever is in your heart, that is what will come out and that is how you will live your life. Change your outlook by dwelling on God's Word and all the great things He is doing. Begin meditating on and confessing what His Word says about your circumstances.

Jesus is doing so many miracles, healings, signs and wonders these days. It is increasing and picking up with greater intensity as time goes by. We need to focus on this! While ministering in Peru in August 2009, we shared about a lady who was healed of breast cancer in it's final stages at our Barielly, India campaign. Her breasts were literally rotting and oozing. The doctors said she needed to have them removed or she would be dead soon. As we shared this testimony in Lima, Peru, it imparted faith to a number of other women who where healed of breast cancer or other forms of cancer.

"...For the testimony of Jesus is the spirit of prophecy" (Revelation 19:10b). When we begin to share the testimonies of Jesus, we are prophesying that He is able to do the same miracle again and again. This principle has worked successfully in our overseas campaigns as we share testimonies of healings Jesus has done in previous campaigns. As people hear these testimonies, their faith is quickened to believe Jesus for a similar miracle for themselves. Here is one report we received after we returned to the USA, from our translator, of how the Lord works through the power of the testimony and dwelling on positive things God is doing:

"..Now, the 84 year old lady who was dying with cancer in our

church and you prayed for. After that night she was taken to the hospital and there she was going again with all the process for cancer treatment. She said to herself: I am tired of being sick, I am not sick, I was prayed for, I don't accept the fact that I am sick, I am not going to die, I don't want to die. And after saying or confessing so. Maybe in a vision or for real, we all don't know, she saw an old man dressed in white with a nice white hat on his head. She wasn't able to see his face, she only remembers seeing him coming and laying his hand on her and then declaring her healing. Then he was gone. After that she asked the doctors where is the man, because she felt that something came out of her and that she was healed.

The doctors thought, she is was having some sort of imagination typical of dying people, along with insanity. Then they decided to make some exams on her, and after 2 times they found out that THERE IS NOT EVEN A DEAD CELL IN HER BODY AND THAT CANCER IS TOTALLY GONE!! They were in shock. Healed by Jesus' stripes."

-Gonzalo Del Aguila, Lima, Peru

All over the world, we are hearing reports about "a man dressed in white" appearing to people just like this older lady testified. In an earthquake in Haiti, people were pulled out the rubble weeks after the earthquake. A couple, when asked how they survived, said "a man dressed in white" was tending to them, keeping them alive, and they had no fear. We are also hearing reports time and time again of Jesus or angels appearing to people and instantly healing them. Many Muslims all over the world are reporting seeing a man dressed in white with nail prints in His hands, making it easy to preach the Gospel to them.

an excellent book, *The Destiny of Islam in the Endtimes*, written by a former Pakistani Muslim, Faisal Malick (published by Destiny Image), the author (now a preacher) shares about a testimony that came on Egyptian news. A missionary had shared it with him. A man killed his wife and buried her. He also buried alive his two daughters, an eight year old and a nursing infant. Fifteen days later, an uncle died and was buried in the same location. When they came to bury the uncle, they found the two girls alive. The TV anchor woman wearing a burka asked how they were still alive. The eight year girl responded saying that every morning a man clothed in white with holes in his hand would come and wake the mother to feed the baby sister. This man also brought food to the older girl. The interviewer said, "This sounds like that man named Jesus we have been hearing about..." Shortly after that the feed to the cameras was cut. Those are the kinds of testimonies we should be dwelling on, because God is moving like never before with miracles, healings, signs and wonders on this earth, *"...With men this is impossible, but with God all things are possible"* (Matthew 19:26).

Many years ago, the Lord showed me that, if I was offended or critical with a ministry or a certain emphasis in the Body of Christ, then I would not be able to receive from them or the anointing on them unless I repented. I have seen the media and believers get easily offended with people like Benny Hinn, for example. They zero in on a small flaw in his life or someone not healed under his ministry, ignoring the many who have been healed.

The enemy knows that if we focus on what God is not doing and remain silent about what God has done, then there will be no reproduction of those miracles. Isaiah 62:6 says, *"You who make mention of the Lord, do not keep silent."* The enemy loves to silence believers and keep them from sharing the testimonies of our great God. He wants us to focus on what he and his demons do more than what God does so he has an environment to keep working his destructive power. Sad to say most believers fall prey to these tactics.

When our focus is on what God has done, Romans 10:17 says, *"So then faith comes by hearing, and hearing by the WORD* (Greek word Rhema- means spoken word) *of God."* Faith and the power to act come into our hearts when we hear what God has done or is doing. It activates faith! It is sad that in many Christian circles there is no mention of the miracles Christ is doing or pressing in for these miracles He longs to do in our midst. It breeds unbelief and reliance on natural abilities instead of faith in God which can activate His miracle working power.

If we act according to the Bible and focus on what God has done and is continuing to do it will get the momentum going for what He desires to do in the future. It's like getting a long train moving. It is slow at first, but once it starts moving one does not want to stop it or get in its way. Just keep that momentum going!

If we focus on the good things God is doing, that becomes the lens through which we see; one could say it becomes our belief system. It becomes the way we perceive God and what He can and will do continually.

Quoted from *Humility The Hidden Key to Walking in Signs and Wonders* published by Destiny Image, Chapter 7 Page 155.

When the Gospel is watered down and miracles and healings are not happening, or they are frowned upon, you will see people walk away from God just like Israel and Judah did in the

Old Testament. Sin will run rampant in an environment like this. Where Jesus is manifesting His presence in signs, wonders and miracles, you will see a people passionately pursuing God.

Joshua 24:31 is a profound statement that holds true today. : "Israel served the Lord all the days of Joshua, and all the days of the elders who outlived Joshua, who had known all the works of the Lord which He had done for Israel." When we become self sufficient and only do what we can work up in the natural, we put God in a box and begin limiting His power. The overall effects are even worse. Multitudes are not reached with the Gospel of Jesus Christ and believers backslide. Yet, many Christians are content because at least they are going to heaven. When Israel forgot the works of the Lord, they also forgot about involving God in the affairs or their everyday lives! Soon they went into idolatry, turned to other gods and immorality. Is it any different today? Many young people who have grown up in churches have turned from Christ because of cold, dead religion that is powerless.

Speaking of Israel, Psalms 78:40-42 says, *"How often they provoked Him in the wilderness, And grieved Him in the desert! Yes, again and again they tempted God, And limited the Holy One of Israel. They did not remember His power: The day when He redeemed them from the enemy."* Let's not be guilty and do the same as Israel did. They began to forget the works of the Lord and soon became dependent only on what they could perceive in the natural. It did not take long after that for the nation as a whole to stray from God. Do not be content with cold, dead religion or self-reliance and forget that with Jesus, nothing is impossible. He is God who created the universe.

PREPARING FOR FAILURE

One of the reasons people do not see miracles and healings on a regular basis is because of the way they believe and their resultant actions. Jesus said in Mark 11:24, *"Therefore I say to you, whatever things you ask when you pray believe that you receive them, and you will have them."* If we really believed this, then once we have made our petitions known to God, we would begin to thank Him for the answer, confessing His faithfulness to answer our prayers and we would prepare to succeed.

Sharmila and I have met some missionary leaders whose motto was "Believe for the best, but prepare for the worst." What a contradiction! The testimony of one couple was plagued with all that went wrong, failures and the difficulties they had on the mission field. Their beliefs definitely paved the way for their negative experiences. Their conclusion on the matter was that God does not promise us anything! I do not know what version of the Bible they read to conclude such heresy. James 1:6-8 says, *"But let him ask in faith, with no doubting, for he who doubts is like a wave of the sea driven and tossed by the wind. For let not that man suppose that he will receive anything from the Lord; he is a double-minded man, unstable in all his ways."* True belief in God means we prepare to succeed at whatever God has called us to do; we believe to receive from God. God will come through! Hebrews 11:6 says, *"But without faith it is impossible to please Him, for he who comes to God must believe that He is, and that He is a rewarder of those who diligently seek Him."*

FEAR, WORRY AND ANXIETY

Job believed wrongly about God and religious tradition tells us God made Job sick. God corrected Job's theology towards the end of the book of Job. The Bible tells us in Job 2:7, *"So Satan went out from the presence of the LORD, and struck Job with painful boils from the sole of his foot to the crown of his head."* Job did not seem to realize there was a devil and demons. He makes no mention of them and accuses God of doing what Satan had done. It is really sad when religious people buy into the lie that God makes us suffer with sickness when all along it is either Satan, his demons or ourselves who are the culprits. What a slap in God's face to accuse Him of causing natural disasters and afflicting people. Fear opened the door for Satan and demons to attack Job. God did not do that to Job. Job 3:25 says, *"For the thing I greatly feared has come upon me, and what I dreaded has happened to me."* The Hebrew literally says, "I feared a fear and it came upon me." Fear can activate Satan's destructive power the same way faith activates God's miracle working power.

In Luke 21:26, Jesus talks about the last days; *"Men's hearts failing them from fear and expectation of those things which are coming on the earth, for the powers of heaven will be shaken."* Men's hearts would fail them because they choose to focus on the negative things happening. Philippians 4:6 says, *"Be anxious for nothing, but in everything by prayer and supplication, with thanksgiving, let your requests be known to God."* Anxiety, worry, stress and fear can cause ulcers, heart problems and other maladies. Jesus told us many times concerning the last days to "Fear not." Jesus exhorts us in Matthew 6:25-34 not to worry because worry will not change our circumstances one iota for the better. Instead of worrying anxiously about tomorrow, He encourages us in verse 33, *"But seek first the kingdom of God and His righteousness, and all these things shall be added to you."* That can include healing, provision or whatever you may need.

Some people do not even realize they are living their lives in fear. Let me explain. They are letting negative experiences from the past dictate how their lives should be lived today. They do not appear to be living in fear outwardly, but by their subconscious actions and decisions they are living in fear. They do not even recognize the decisions they are making today are controlled by fear from what they have experienced in the past. It can greatly impact the lives of those that are close to them by passing on those fears and phobias. Fear is contagious just like faith is contagious.

Faith needs to be the center of our decision making process. Do not let fears and phobias from the past control your future destiny. Notice how many times Jesus and angels said "Fear not." They said this knowing fear is a destructive force in a person's life. Fear is faith perverted. It is putting faith in what the Devil has said about your circumstances. Put faith in God's Word not what the Devil, demons or your physical circumstances dictate.

Notice these promises in the Word: *"The Lord is on my side; I will not fear. What can man do to me?"* (Psalms 118:6). Jesus said, *"Behold, I give you the authority to trample on serpents and scorpions, and over all the power of the enemy, and nothing shall by any means hurt you."* (Luke 10:19). This is Jesus' promise to you, nothing shall harm you. If He is on our side and has given us this promise we can in faith effectively wage war on fear.

I remember a time early in our marriage when we were traveling to Colorado to attend a conference, be interviewed on radio and speak at a church. We were driving an old car. In those days I remember having brief moments where I was fearful of death or being permanently injured in an accident. While Sharmila was driving just south of Buffalo, Wyoming on I-25 it appeared that the steering column on the car collapsed. Sharmila lost control of the car; it rolled a number of times and end up facing oncoming traffic in the northbound lane of I-25. The roof caved in on my head making me a little shorter. People who witnessed this accident thought for sure we were both dead. The car was totaled. Sharmila sprained her ankle, but otherwise we came away with only minor scraps and needed a few stitches. .

While the car was rolling I remember having such a peace. It was God's grace! He said nothing shall by any means hurt you. He meant what he said. The ambulance came and picked us up. We were treated in the local hospital and released. Sharmila prayed over me as I felt compacted and my chest was feeling pressure. I sat down in a chair and she commanded my leg to come back out even with the other leg in Jesus' name. Instantly it shot out and I was healed and back to my original height. We had no money for another automobile at that time. The Lord came through and provided the money for a used van two days later. Since that time, I have never feared death or being permanently disabled. I put faith in His word for divine protection. As we travel a lot, we depend on His protection at all times. We have had other close calls, but each time He has given angels charge over us (Psalms 91:11) and we have been protected. It pays to walk by faith!

BLAMING GOD FOR YOUR PROBLEMS

Too often when problems come our way, people make God responsible. Much of this belief was passed on from Augustine and John Calvin who believed God did both good and evil things to people. Many blame God for every catastrophe in their lives. It is either ourselves, mankind or Satan and his demons bringing these calamities upon us. God is not the author of sickness, infirmities or calamities in our lives. He is the one who turns it around for the better. Insurance companies call natural disasters "acts of God"; that is so far from the truth. James 1:17 says, *"Every good and every perfect gift is from above, and comes down from the Father of lights, with whom there is no variation or shadow of turning."* God's nature is such that He is only capable of bringing good into our lives.

When we hold God responsible for our problems, we close the door to freedom from those problems. It is Satan's intense desire to make us point the finger at God, and staying bound by our problems. Acts 10:38 says, *"How God anointed Jesus of Nazareth with the Holy Spirit and power, who went about doing good and healing all who were oppressed by the devil, for God was with Him."* This scripture makes it so apparent that God anointed Jesus to do good. Jesus said in John 10:10, *"the thief* (Satan and demons) *does not come except to steal, and to kill, and to destroy. I have come that they may have life, and that they may have it more abundantly."*

DEPRESSION

Nehemiah 8:10 says, *"The joy of the Lord is your strength."* Joy, the opposite of depression, is part of the fruit of the spirit. If the devil can steal your joy, then he can also steal your goods, but if you can be joyful irrespective of the circumstances then you can hold on to your health, finances and have victory in every area of your life (Hebrews 10:32-36).

Proverbs 17:22 says, *"A merry heart does good like a medicine, but a broken spirit dries the bones."* Depression can bring bone or joint problems like arthritis. Joy is akin to medicine. It is also a good barometer that tells us if we are trusting God or not. Joy helps us see with eyes of faith to the end of the trial. Hebrews 12:2 says, *"Looking unto Jesus, the author and finisher of our faith, who for the joy set before Him endured the cross, despising the shame, and has sat down at the right hand of the throne of God."* Jesus endured the cross because He could see the end result of His trial. When we allow depression to creep into our lives, we are permitting the devil to walk all over us and to blind us from the destiny God has for us. Isaiah 61:3 says, *"to console those who mourn in Zion, to give them beauty for ashes, the oil of joy for mourning, the garment of praise for the spirit of heaviness...".* When we are ungrateful, depression and unhappiness follow. That can be a breeding ground for unbelief, sickness and disease. Notice Deuteronomy 28:47, *"Because you did not serve the Lord with your God with joy and gladness of heart, for the abundance of everything...".* This was part of the curse, when every calamity that could come upon a person would come because of lack of thankfulness and joy.

A PERSON'S FREE WILL

Just as the centurion gave Jesus permission or authority to pray for his sick servant in Luke 7:1-10, we need permission (authority) to pray for or share with the sick. If a person does not give us authority to pray or share with them, it can be a detriment to healing. Healing does not manifest itself when the person concerned does not desire healing, as was the case with my father-in-law, Major David Frank, who went to be with Jesus on May 2, 2006. For the most part Jesus does not violate a person's free will. We were earnestly praying for David to be healed, when all he wanted was to go home. He told his wife, Renuka, months in advance that he was leaving soon, and she would do a good job when he left. He prepared her for his homegoing. He spent his last year disconnected from this world, worshipping Jesus, waiting on the Lord, reading the Word or praying. He never once prayed to live, but instead called upon the Lord constantly to take him home when death was close by.

A year earlier he had been healed supernaturally of a cardiac arrest where only 5% of his heart was functioning. During his stay in the hospital, he saw glimpses of heaven. Jesus also appeared to him and told him He had work for him to do and healed him. He proceeded to organize a large campaign for us on the India/Pakistan border, right after a major earthquake. After that, he spent time training my mother-in-law on how to set up a campaign and deal with the finances. His sole desire was to be with Jesus in heaven after that. The doctors do not know why he died. They said his heart simply stopped beating.

INSENSITIVITY TO THE HOLY SPIRIT

"Nevertheless I tell you the truth. It is to your advantage that I go away; for if I do not go away, the Helper will not come to you; but if I depart, I will send Him to you. And when He has come, He will convict the world of sin, and of righteousness, and of judgment: of sin, because they do not believe in Me; of righteousness, because I go to My Father and you see Me no more; of judgment, because the ruler of this world is judged.

"I still have many things to say to you, but you cannot bear them now. However, when He, the Spirit of truth, has come, He will guide you into all truth; for He will not speak on His own authority, but whatever He hears He will speak; and He will tell you things to come. He will glorify Me, for He will take of what is Mine and declare it to you. All things that the Father has are Mine. Therefore I said that He will take of Mine and declare it to you" (John 16:7-15).

First off, notice how many times Jesus refers to the Holy Spirit as a person in the above verses. Yet in many Christian circles, the Holy Spirit (God) is given little or no attention. The Holy

Spirit helps carry out the present day ministry of Jesus. Look at Acts 10:38, how *"God anointed Jesus of Nazareth with the Holy Spirit and with power, who went about doing good and healing all who were oppressed by the devil, for God was with Him."* The same Holy Spirit is available to every believer today to carry out the healing ministry of Jesus. Many believers have become insensitive to His moving or leading. Jesus was dependent on the Holy Spirit and taught us to be dependent on the Holy Spirit to carry out the works He did. *"Most assuredly, I say to you, he who believes in Me, the works that I do he will do also; and greater works than these he will do, because I go to My Father. And whatever you ask in My name, that I will do, that the Father may be glorified in the Son. If you ask anything in My name, I will do it"* (John 14:12-13). What happened when Jesus went to the Father? He poured out the Holy Spirit upon all who want to walk in fellowship and intimacy with Him.

The Holy Spirit is referred to as a dove. Doves are very skittish birds. If a dove was resting on your shoulder, you would be very careful how you walked so the dove would stay with you. We should treat the Holy Spirit the same way if we want to learn to flow with Him in the miracles and healings of Jesus.

My mother was dying of cancer in 1974. Around that time she had heard things about the baptism of the Holy Spirit, but as a good Lutheran decided that was not for her. One night she was taken up to heaven and heard the most beautiful worship she had ever heard. She heard people and angels in heaven singing praises to God in tongues. After that experience, she opened her heart, was baptized in the Holy Spirit, received her heavenly prayer language and also learned what the Word of God said concerning divine healing. My mom and dad began standing on

God's Word for her healing. During one of her check ups, the doctors came into her room and said, "there is a mystery that has taken place in your blood cells and you do not have cancer anymore." She has never had another problem with cancer again.

The Holy Spirit is referred to as a "Helper" (Greek - standby). He is an ever-present help in the time of danger, calamity and sickness to help pull us out of that mess.

Much sickness strikes when our immune system is run down. In recent years, Dr. Carl Peterson, a brain specialist at Oral Roberts University, conducted research on the relationship between the brain and praying in the Holy Spirit (praying in tongues -Mark 16:17). He discovered that as we engage in praying in the Spirit, the brain releases two chemical secretions that are directed into our immune systems, giving a 35-40% boost to our immune system. It produces healing within our bodies. This secretion is triggered from a part of the brain that has no other activity in humans. The baptism of the Holy Spirit with the evidence of speaking in tongues just like the early church received in the Acts 2:1-4, 10:44-48, and 19:1-6 is available to all believers in Jesus. Right before ascending into heaven and pouring out the Holy Spirit in Acts 1:8 Jesus said, *"But you shall receive power (Greek-miraculous ability) when the Holy Spirit has come upon you; and you shall be witnesses to Me in Jerusalem, and in all Judea and Samaria, and to the end of the earth."*

Acts 2:38-39 says, *"Then Peter said to them, "Repent, and let every one of you be baptized in the name of Jesus Christ for the remission of sins; and you shall receive the gift of the Holy Spirit. For the promise is to you and to your children, and to all who are afar off, as many as the Lord our God will call."* The baptism of the Holy Spirit is what turned my life around and thrust me into a world-wide healing ministry where we have seen hundreds of thousands turn to Christ as we have witnessed the miracle working power of Jesus time and time again. I also believe that is why my family remains very healthy. The Holy Spirit is our source of health and wholeness. The baptism of the Holy Spirit is an experience available to all, as mentioned in the above verses, which takes place after salvation. All you have do is hunger and ask for it and Jesus will baptize you in the Holy Spirit. It was one of the most powerful experiences I have ever had. That experience radically changed my life, gave me a passion for lost souls, direction and it can for you also.

CHAPTER 4

THE IMPORTANCE OF FAITH

"Now the next day, when they had come out from Bethany, He was hungry. And seeing from afar a fig tree having leaves, He went to see if perhaps he would find something on it. When He came to it, He found nothing but leaves, for it was not the season for figs. In response Jesus said to it, Let no one eat fruit from you ever again. And His disciples heard it...Now in the morning, as they passed by, they saw the fig tree dried up from the roots. And Peter remembering, said to Him, Rabbi look! The fig tree which You cursed has withered away. So Jesus answered and said to them, Have faith in God. For assuredly, I say to you, whoever says to this mountain, Be removed and be cast into the sea, and does not doubt in his heart, but believes that those things he says will be done, he will have whatever he says. Therefore I say to you, whatever things you ask when you pray, believe that you receive them, and you will have them. And whenever you stand praying, if you have anything against anyone, forgive him, that your Father in heaven may also forgive you your trespasses. But if you do not forgive, neither will

your Father in heaven forgive your trespass (Mark 11:12- 14, 20-26).

We can learn a lot about road blocks to healing from these passages. Notice that Jesus cursed the fig tree from the roots (vs. 14 and 20), but nothing happened immediately, at least not in the natural realm. Those who heard and saw Jesus curse the fig tree may have wondered what He was doing. Many try to deal with the surface issues or symptoms of the problem, rather than getting to the root. Doing this will never produce lasting freedom. All they will be able to do is learn to cope with their problems. Jesus dealt with the root in teaching us the principles of real faith and walking in victory.

In verse 21, Peter was astonished that the tree had withered away from the roots. Jesus cursed the fig tree to show His disciples how faith works. One of the primary hindrances to healing is not dealing with the root issues of a problem. We will cover some in this teaching.

NOT HAVING FAITH

In verse 22, Jesus says, *"have faith in God."* The original Greek version is *"have the faith of God."* You can have the faith of God to help you when you are going through problems with your health. It goes much further than our own faith.

You can also gather from the ensuing four verses that faith does not operate by the five physical senses. We should never separate the spiritual and physical realms. They work together. Faith affects the spiritual realm, which has preeminence over the physical realm. It is for this reason that Paul says in 2 Corinthians 5:7, *"For we walk by faith, not by sight."*

One will never grasp and tap into the enormity of faith and miracles if one is governed by their five physical senses, rather than faith in God's promises. Being ruled by the five senses can be a hindrance or road block to healing. In Verse 23, Jesus tells us to speak to the mountain (problems) before us and it will be removed. He does not tell us to ignore the problem. It is essential that we acknowledge it and confront it with faith in Him.

It is interesting that in this verse Jesus repeatedly says you will have what you say. If you desire to walk in faith, then you need to understand the power of your words or tongue. Proverbs 18:21 says, *"Death and life are in the power of the tongue, And those who love it will eat its fruit."* Negative confessions speaking contrary to God's will is another hindrance to healing. James 3:6 says your *"tongue sets on fire the course of nature."* Our words have power. When we speak and confess God's word with a heart full of faith, we can change our negative circumstances. Jesus said, *"For assuredly, I say to you, whoever says to this mountain, 'Be removed and be cast into the sea,' and does not doubt in his heart, but believes that those things he says will be done, he will have whatever he says"* (Mark 11:23). Here's the problem; many believers speak negatively and end receiving the negative things they speak. We should speak and quote God's word.

According to verse 24, when should we believe we receive what we pray for? The minute we pray! It is immaterial whether we see it or feel it immediately! Faith says it is as good as answered because God said it. One way to determine if we are walking by faith is to examine how we apply this verse to our lives. Do we really believe we have received? In that case, we should cease begging God and continually petitioning God to answer our prayer. We should begin confessing His Word regarding our circumstances, praising Him for hearing and answering our prayers.

If I have a problem before me, like a sickness or financial need, and I pray, if my prayer is answered instantly, do I need faith for those needs to be met? Of course not! When is faith needed? When we do not see the answer in the natural realm! Faith in God and His promises releases His miracle working power, affecting the spiritual realm, then the natural realm. Many give up if healing does not happen immediately, not understanding how faith operates.

Many stop at verse 24, not realizing that verse 25 and 26 are key to walking and living by faith as well. If we walk in unforgiveness, offense or have a critical attitude, we can literally short-circuit our faith and our miracle. If we are easily offended and have a critical attitude or unforgiveness, our faith may never get out of the chute. These negatives will hinder the blessings of God in our lives.

This is a very crucial hindrance to healing that we find in verse 25-26. Bitterness, anger, unforgiveness, offense and judgement can literally be an open door to the destructive power of the Satan and his demons. A person full of these attitudes will have a hard time being joyous and thankful, not realizing the power of thankfulness and joy. Proverbs 17:22 says, *"A merry* (also thankful) *heart does good, like a medicine, but a broken spirit dries the bones."*

Hebrews 12:14-15 says, *"Pursue peace with all people, and holiness, without which no one will see the Lord: looking carefully lest anyone fall short of the grace of God, lest any root of bitterness springing up cause trouble, and by this many become defiled."* When we hold on to bitterness, it can literally poison us physically, mentally and spiritually. Many medical studies show that anger, unforgiveness and bitterness can actually release toxins and compromise our immune system making one more susceptible to illnesses like cancer or arthritis. It will spring up like a weed and destroy the fruit of the Spirit in our life. It all starts with offense. Once given place, it destroys our judgment and discernment. Offense rapidly turns to bitterness, which in turn can spread to the rest of our body and the body of Christ defiling many to the point of making us ineffective for Christ.

Bitterness, the critical spirit and offense is a "fungus among us." If unchecked, it grows like a fungus, consuming the entire person. We need to lay the axe to the root of the problems, not just the surface issues (that often invites our problems back at a later time in life). An excellent book on the subject is *The Bait of Satan*, by John Bevere published by Charisma House.

UNCONFESSED SIN

"If I regard iniquity in my heart, the Lord will not hear me." (Psalm 66:18). Unconfessed sin can prevent the flow of God's healing anointing. If we really love Christ and claim to be mature Christians, it is unacceptable for us to hang on to unconfessed sins. Proverbs 28:13 says, *"He who covers his sin will not prosper, but whoever confesses and forsakes them will have mercy."* Did you know that true prosperity is not just financial, but the ability of God within us to meet any need, spiritual, mental, physical or financial? When we cover our sins and refuse to deal with them, then we can literally give demons an open door into our lives, preventing the free flow of God's provision. All we need to do is repent and fall out of agreement with that sin (James 5:14-15 & 1 John 1:9).

We learn from Old Testament examples that when Israel or Judah sinned and refused to repent, they came under a severe curse. Once they repented and came back to God, blessings would begin to rain down on them (Deuteronomy 28). So many Christians go overboard in this area. They believe that when healing does not manifest immediately, it is because of lack of faith or sin. This is, however, not always the case and an easy cop out. Look at John 9:1: *"Now as Jesus passed by, He saw a man who was born blind from birth. And His disciples asked Him, saying Rabbi, who sinned, this man or his parents, that he was born blind?"* Not really a smart question if you think about it! It would be pretty hard to sin before you are born. This was the ungodly religious attitude in Jesus' day. Notice Jesus' response to the incorrect thinking: *"Neither this man nor his parents sinned, but that the works of God should be revealed in him"* (John 9:2). Then Jesus proceeded to open his eyes.

ARROGANCE

"Do not be wise in your own eyes; fear the Lord and, depart from evil. It will be health (Hebrew – medicine) *to your flesh and strength* (Hebrew-marrow, refreshment) *to your bones"* (Proverbs 3:7-8). Fleeing from pride, arrogance and walking in humility can be medicine to our flesh, strength and refreshment to our bones. Think about the doing the opposite of these verses. Could that cause health problems?

"But He gives more grace. Therefore He says: GOD RESISTS (Greek: ranges in battle against) *the proud but gives grace to humble."* (James 4:6) The humble are recipients of God's grace. Jesus commented only on two occasions that someone had "great faith." The centurion whose servant needed healing in Luke 7:1-10 and the Canaanite woman, who's daughter was demonized in

Matthew 15:21-28! Both received their miracle and both understood the importance of humility in relation to receiving healing from Christ.

The story of Namaan, commander of the Syrian army and a very prideful man, is another lesson in humility. We can read this story in 2 Kings 5:1-19. Pride angered him, preventing him from obeying the advice of Elisha's servant. He nearly missed out on his miracle because of his arrogance. However, once he humbled himself (at his servant's suggestion) and immersed himself in the river Jordan seven times, he was instantly healed of his leprosy.

In 32 years of ministry, there have been occasions when I have witnessed arrogance and pride stop healings in our meetings. The pride, criticalness and offense stemmed the flow of God's power in these meetings (Mark 6:1-6). There have also been occasions when I have been prideful and God has resisted me and I would see no or very few miracles in my meetings. I did not even realize the cause for it. How many Christians have missed out on their miracles because of pride? I tend to think multitudes!

2 Chronicles 7:14 says, *"If my people who are called by My name will humble themselves, and pray and seek my face and turn from their wicked ways* (deal with root issues in their lives, not just surface issues), *then I will hear from Heaven and I will forgive their sin and heal their land."* This talks of a permanent healing. The first thing we need to address for God to bring healing to our land and us personally is to humble ourselves!

If you would like to know more about humility and its relationship to healing, signs and wonders, you can order my book *Humility: The Hidden Key to Walking in Signs and Wonders* (published by Destiny Image).

CHAPTER 5

WHAT WAS PAUL'S THORN IN THE FLESH?

There are other hindrances to healing that we need to avoid mentioned in the Bible. These pitfalls in our lives can prevent healing from flowing freely. A belief in physical suffering can also stop healing.

"and lest I should be exalted above measure by the abundance of the revelations, a thorn in the flesh was given to me, a messenger of Satan to buffet me, lest I be exalted above measure. Concerning this thing I pleaded with the Lord three times that it might depart from me. And He said to me, 'My grace is sufficient for you, for My strength is made perfect in weakness.' Therefore most gladly I will rather boast in my infirmities, that the power of Christ may rest upon me. Therefore I take pleasure in infirmities, in reproach, in needs in persecutions, in distress, for Christ's sake. For when I am weak, then I am strong" (2 Corinthians 12:7-10).

There has been a lot of controversy in Christian circles over these scriptures, concerning Paul's thorn in the flesh. Many feel that we have to remain sick to glorify God in our physical weakness. Much of that belief comes from the influence of Greek philosophy and asceticism (a belief in suffering physically to get closer to God) mixed with Christianity in the early days of Christianity. Many have gone to premature graves because of this incorrect belief. In this chapter, we want to share through God's word, exactly what Paul's thorn in the flesh was.

Many Christians have experiences and then try to make a doctrine out of those experiences. If our experiences do not line up with the Word of God, we cannot make a doctrine of it; God's Word should be first place. When we can get to the point of trusting God's Word first and foremost, then our experiences will end up lining up with the Word, not contradicting it.

WHAT RELIGIOUS TRADITION BELIEVES PAUL'S THORN WAS

In 2 Corinthians chapter 12, Paul received a thorn in the flesh as a result of the revelation he saw. Many feel they have received a thorn in the flesh as well. Have they received a revelation so great and been caught up to Heaven as Paul was? This is what brought on the thorn in the flesh (2 Corinthians 12:1-6).

A number of people believe that Paul's thorn was a sickness. Some believe that Paul's thorn was an eye disease that the Lord refused to heal. If that was the case, then Paul was the first person in the New Testament who the Lord refused to heal. Acts 10:38 says, *"God anointed Jesus of Nazareth with the Holy Ghost and power, who went about doing good and healing all who were oppressed by the devil, for God was with Him."* Only once in the New Testament Jesus was unable to heal the sick: Matthew 13:58, *"He did not many mighty works because of their unbelief."*

People quote Galatians 4:13-15, to prove that Paul's thorn in the flesh was an eye disease. It reads: *"You know that because of physical infirmity I preached the gospel to you at first. And my trial which was in my flesh you did not despise or reject, but you received me as an angel of God even as Christ Jesus. What then was the blessing you enjoyed? For I bear you witness that, if possible, you would have plucked out your own eyes and given them to me."* The word infirmity in the original Greek means bodily infirmity, such as mentioned in 2 Corinthians 11:23-30, not a disease. Paul had been physically beaten many times for preaching the gospel and suffered with physical infirmities because of it. However, I am sure God healed him each time, as He does today. The Lord even raised Paul from the dead in Acts 14:19-21. Galatians 4:15 in no way shows that Paul had an eye disease. The Galatians were friendly with Paul at that time and would have given Paul anything he needed, hence Paul writes that you would have given me your eyes if I had needed them. It does not say that he had an eye disease. Paul was merely using that as an example, saying that the Galatians were really committed to him and cared deeply for him and his needs to be met. There is no mention of any eye disease in these verses.

For the sake of argument, lets assume that Paul did have an eye disease and that was the reason why the power of God rested on him. If that was the case, we should all pray and ask God to make us sick so we can be greatly anointed. We should not go to a doctor, but suffer in our sickness to glorify God as well. That is absurd, but that is the way many Christians believe because of the Greek influence, gnosticism and asceticism that was mingled with early Christianity.

After reading what the Word of God says on healing, how

healing was provided in the atonement at Calvary, I do not see how anyone could believe that remaining sick glorifies God. (Isaiah 53:4-5, Matthew 8:16-17, 1 Peter 2:24) John 6:2 says, *"Then a great multitude followed Him* (Jesus), *Because they saw His signs which He performed on those who were diseased."* Acts 3-5 tells us that many thousands turned to Jesus because of the miraculous healings that took place when the disciples preached about the risen Jesus and prayed for the sick and infirm. No one turned to Jesus because of some disciple remaining sick to show patience and fortitude! Many turned to Jesus because of the healings and miracles He performed on those that were suffering.

MESSENGER OF SATAN

2 Corinthians 12:7 clearly shows us what Paul's thorn in the flesh was. It says it was the messenger of Satan. The word messenger appears seven times in the Bible and the word angel appears 181 times. Both words come from the Greek word *angelos,* which means messenger or angel. They can be used interchangeably. Hence we see that the thorn in the flesh was a personality, a demonic angel rather than an eye disease.

Numbers 33:55 sheds more light on the subject. It says that the inhabitants of the land (or other nations) would be pricks in Israel's eyes and thorns in their sides, and would vex them in the land wherein they dwelt if they would not drive them out. They would not physically be pricks in their eyes or physical thorns in their sides, but just like a thorn in the side is an annoyance, the other nations would be an annoyance to the Israelites. Joshua 23:11-13 and 2 Samuel 23:6 both talk about thorns, but both refer to a personality rather than a sickness or disease.

WEAKNESSES AND INFIRMITIES

2 Corinthians 12:9 tells us that this messenger of Satan (Paul's thorn) caused "weaknesses" or "infirmities" to come upon Paul. The words weaknesses and infirmities can also be used interchangeably. The Greek word is 'astheneia' according to Thayers Greek-English Lexicon means "weakness and to bear trials and troubles." Once again, it has no reference to sickness or disease. 2 Corinthians 12:9 reads, *"and He said to me, 'My* (Christ's) *grace* (which is for the inner man or spirit) *is sufficient for you, for My strength is made perfect in weakness* (Greek- asthenia).' *Therefore most gladly I will rather boast in my infirmities, that the power of Christ may rest upon me."* The weakness mentioned here does not refer to physical weakness, as in sickness, but one's own spiritual weakness. When we realize that in and of ourselves we are weak, but God is strong, then we will see the power of God resting on us. Paul realized that apart from Jesus, he could do nothing (John 15:5).

Paul also said that he would glory in these trials and troubles, the reason being that, when everything is always nice and comfortable, many tend to sit back and take it easy, depending more on self than the Lord. I can testify on this in my own life - when trials have come, I have to exercise faith to get through those trials or I will not make it. Trials have often caused me to press in more. When there are struggles, I have to exercise faith and my faith grows because I have to stand on God's Word to see me through. Sometimes the true test to see what I have comes under pressure. That is why it is important to have an unshakable foundation in God's Word.

THE ONLY SUFFERING WE ARE CALLED TO ENDURE

I do not see anywhere in God's Word where He has called anyone to suffer with sickness or disease. There are times He has called us to suffer. 2 Timothy 2:12 says, *"if we suffer with Him (Jesus) we will reign with Him."* This is not talking about sickness; it is talking about persecution for standing up for the name of Jesus. 2 Timothy 3:12 says, *"all who live godly in Christ shall suffer persecution."* [5]

WHAT DID PAUL'S THORN CAUSE?

I have shared with you what Paul's thorn is not and have explained the thorn in the flesh. I want to share with you what Paul's thorn in the flesh caused to happen to him.

2 Corinthians 11:23-30, the verses just before, talking about Paul's thorn, clearly reveals that Paul's thorn in the flesh was a messenger or angel (demon) of Satan that caused Paul to go through beatings, prison, shipwrecks, death, weariness, hunger, thirst, cold, nakedness, painfulness and many other perils. Nowhere does it say that Paul's thorn was an eye disease or sickness. We need to stick to God's word. If it is not in the Word, then do not buy into that belief. That is how false doctrine comes about.

In 2 Corinthians 11:29-30, Paul sums it up by saying, *"Who is weak, and I am not weak? Who is made to stumble, and I do not burn with indignation? If I must boast, I will boast in the things which concern my infirmity."* Paul did not glory in sickness. He gloried in that he had to bear trials and troubles while he was taking a stand for Jesus.

[5] *Matthew 5:10-12, Mark 10:29-30, Luke 6:26, John 15:20, Acts 5:41-42 concerning suffering and persecution when standing up for Jesus and witnessing to the lost.*

Acts 5 talks about the miracles that God did through the apostles as they preached Jesus Christ and the persecution they suffered. Acts 5:41-42 records, *"So they departed from the presence of the council, rejoicing that they were counted worthy to suffer shame for His name. And daily in the temple, and in every house, they did not cease teaching and preaching Jesus as the Christ."* If you believe you are to suffer for God's glory consider what it is to suffer for Him while out preaching the Gospel of Jesus Christ not with sickness. Suffering with sickness is not what glorifies God. The glory goes to God when we believe in God for a miracle and we receive it. The scriptures are very clear on this.[6]

Isaiah 53:4-5, Matthew 8:16-17 and 1 Peter 2:24 all talk about Christ bearing our sins, griefs, sorrows, sickness, disease and infirmities. If that is true, why are so many Christians thinking they have to bear sickness, infirmities and disease? Was not Christ's suffering and sacrifice enough? It was more than enough! I am going to stand for what Jesus purchased! Jesus Christ paid for it all! It belongs to you. You do not have to suffer with these things to glorify God. Jesus bore our sin, sickness, torment, poverty, and humiliation—not with us, but for us! He is not asking us to bear or carry these things. He did it for us. The word borne in Isaiah 53:4 is the Hebrew word nasa, which means "suffered for, bear up, carry off, take away." He did all the suffering so we do not have to. He took the raw deal and we received the good deal. He paid the price in full for spirit, soul and body.

CONCLUSION

In Romans 8:26 it says, *"Likewise the Spirit also helps in our weaknesses (asthenia). For we do not know what we should pray*

---

[6] *John 9, Mark 2:1-12, Matthew 9:1-8, Matthew 15:29-31, Luke 7:11-17, Luke 17:11-19, Luke 18:35-43*

for as we ought, but the spirit Himself makes intercession for us with groanings which cannot be uttered." Just like Paul, we have someone to depend on when we go through trials and troubles: the Holy Spirit! This is why Paul said in 1 Corinthians 14:18, *"I thank my God, I speak in tongues more than you all."* Paul prayed in tongues because he knew the Holy Spirit would intercede through him according to God's perfect will when he went through those trials. (Romans 8:27-28) He also knew that *"many are the afflictions* (Hebrew word: Ra- adversities and troubles) *of the righteous: but the Lord delivers him out of them all"* (Psalm 34:19).

CHAPTER 6

HAVING DONE ALL TO STAND; KEEP STANDING

Another roadblock to healing is believers not understanding how to stand for what rightfully belongs to them.

"Finally my brethren, be strong in the Lord and in the power of His might. Put on the whole armor of God, that you may be able to (1) stand against the wiles of the devil. For we do not wrestle against flesh and blood, but against powers, against the rulers of the darkness of this age, against spiritual hosts of wickedness in the heavenly places. Therefore take up the whole armor of God, that you may be (2) able to withstand in the evil day, and (3) having done all to stand. (4) Stand therefore..." (Ephesians 6:10-14).

During March 2002, while doing a campaign in Yamunanagar, India, in the midst of immense opposition, we saw the Holy Spirit come forth in a powerful way. Many demoniacs were set free and many miracles took place. It was during this time that the Lord laid this message on my heart. The above verses refer to four ways in which one can stand. Many do not realize that is promised us through His awesome grace can many ialize only by walking or standing in Faith and trust His word. Hebrews 11:6 says, *"But without faith it is impossible to please Him, for he who comes to God must believe that He is, and that He is a rewarder of those who diligently seek Him."* Faith activates the miracle working power and grace of God. We cannot work up His promises (Romans 3:27). We have to believe for miracles and act upon His word.

Many people believe for miracles in their bodies without grasping the concept that faith is a stand and that sometimes a fight is involved to get what rightfully belongs to us. 1 Timothy 6:12 says to *"fight the good fight of Faith…"*. I have spoken to many Christians who were healed miraculously, only to lose it later. I have talked to others who were not healed miraculously and gave up because it did not occur instantly. For a successful Christian walk, it is of fundamental importance to understand how to stand for what rightfully belongs to us.

(1) STANDING AGAINST

Ephesians 6:11 first refers to standing against the wiles (Greek: lies, strategies) of the devil and his demons. How and what are we to stand against? We are standing against demons, their lies and schemes. How do we stand against demonic lies? By applying the truth of God's word! Jesus said in Matthew 24:35, *"Heaven and earth will pass away, but My Words will by no means pass away."* Jesus said He is the truth (John 14:6) and that His word is truth (John 17:17). We need an unwavering trust in the word of God. Luke 1:37 in the Amplified Bible reads *"No word from God is without power or impossible of fulfillment."* The only way Satan and his demons can cause us to stumble and miss out on what God has promised us is by lying to us and we in turn believe those lies and act on what Satan speaks to us. We should adhere to what Evangelist Smith Wigglesworth said, "If God said it, I believe it, that settles it." This gentleman had a phenomenal healing ministry. In fact, it also stands as one of the most powerful healing ministries of the 20th century. He raised scores of people from the dead. He simply believed what God's word said and acted upon it.

It is very clear in scripture that it is God's irrevocable will to heal and deliver. Keep in mind what James 1:17 says, *"Every good and every perfect gift is from above, and comes down from the Father of lights with whom there is no variations or shadow of turning."* God is not the author of sickness, infirmities, poverty, torment, etc. Acts 10:38 records, *"How God anointed Jesus with the Holy Spirit and power, who went about doing good healing ALL who were oppressed by the devil, for God was with Him."*

Truth sets captives free! The enemy's lies bind and blind us when we believe them and build our lives upon them. Jesus said in John 8:31-32, *"If you abide in my word* (truth) *you are My disciples indeed. And you shall know the truth and the truth shall make you free."*

When a disease or infirmity comes upon us, the truth or the fact is that we are suffering with a negative condition, but God's truth is higher than that negative circumstance or fact. As we abide in and continue in His word, then truth will set us free of that problem! In order to do this, the word will need to go from our head to being imbedded in our hearts and spoken out of our mouths. God's word is Spiritual truth. It supersedes physical facts. It can change physical facts by simply applying spiritual truth: God's word to your circumstances.

Romans 12:2 says, *"Do not be conformed* (Greek: fashioned, patterned) *to this world, but be transformed* (Greek: metamorphosis, change from one form to another) *by the renewing of your mind, that you may prove what is the good and acceptable and perfect will of God."* His perfect will is in His word. First, we learn to stand against the enemy by walking in the truth of God's word. Isaiah 55:11 says that God's word *"shall not return to me* (God) *void* (Hebrew: empty, useless), *but it shall accomplish what I please and it shall prosper in the thing for which I sent it."* We cannot go wrong waging war on the enemy by standing on the truth of God's word.

(2) WITHSTAND

Ephesians 6:13 exhorts us to withstand in the evil day (Greek: evil things, hardship, perils, annoyances, causing pain, trouble and physically bad conditions). To withstand in Greek means to resist, set oneself against and to oppose. When the enemy comes knocking on our door with trouble, physical ailments, etc, we should resist and oppose him rather than giving in by accepting the hardship as a part of life.

1 Peter 5:8-9 says, *"Be sober, be vigilant, because your adversary, the devil walks about like a roaring lion, seeking whom he may devour, resist* (Greek- to set one's self against, to withstand, resist, oppose and set against) *him, steadfast in the faith, knowing that the same sufferings are experienced by your brotherhood in the world."* Notice the word resist here. How are we to resist the enemy's attacks? By Faith! Ephesians 6:16 says that the shield of faith will quench all the fiery darts of the wicked one.

Notice the masquerade of the enemy here! He walks about like a roaring lion! All he can offer is a cheap imitation or a perversion of the real truth. The devil is not a roaring lion. .. an imposter! Jesus is the real lion of the tribe of Judah. Proverbs 28:1 says, *"The righteous are as bold as a lion."* The only way Satan can get us is when we doubt God's word and truth. Remember his lies bind and blind us when we act on them.

If the devil says, "you are going to die of this sickness", how do we combat him? By resisting him and standing on God's Word! Understand, when he attacks and lies to us, saying we will not make it, it is only because our answer is on the way.

Theresa Stoner understood what it was to resist the enemy when she was afflicted with lymphatic cancer. In April of 2002, I was asked to conduct a healing service in Grand Junction, Colorado. Theresa came to the healing service that night. In Theresa's words:

That night Mark called for those who needed healing in specific areas to come up and I was one of the first. He had said the Holy Spirit had told him someone with my problem, lymphatic cancer, was there. He and Sharmila laid hands on me and the Holy Spirit moved mightily to heal me. The pressure left my neck and throat. I felt energy I had not had in a long time. For the rest of the service I felt as though I had gravel draining down my throat and that pressure was being lifted from all over my head, neck, and shoulders. I was filled with joy and freedom. I wanted to dance.

After being healed supernaturally by God, the enemy tried to attack her with the cancer again. Theresa, in her own words:

The devil, several times starting the next day, put symptoms of pressure on my throat, stabs of pain, etc, but I was quick to rebuke him and the symptoms left. I never expected Mark and

Sharmila to be in my church that Sunday. He moved miracu-lously through their anointed ministry to preserve my life for His glory, my family's needs and my joy.

Theresa understood that sometimes faith is a fight and fought the fight of faith for her life and healing. She came out victorious in Jesus' name. God will do the same for you if you do not pas-sively give into the attacks of the enemy, but withstand or resist him. James 4:7 says, *"Submit to God. Resist the devil and he will flee from you."*

While building our home/ministry office in 2001, I injured my shoulder from the continual heavy lifting of logs and walls. I received prayer for the problem but there seem to be little change. Finally, at a Peter Youngren meeting in Denver, Colorado, I was completely healed. I returned home and lifted heavy things over my head with no problem. I threw the football to my son with no problem. I played basketball and could shoot the ball with no discomfort.

A short time after my healing, I was playing basketball and my shoulder felt great. My game was far from great, though. While I was playing, the symptoms returned and I could feel the pain again. I quickly rebuked the enemy and said, "You are not taking my healing away." I confessed God's word and immedi-ately I was healed again. Since that day I have had no problem whatsoever with my shoulder.

Many give up on healing if the problems return because they have not learned to stand when the enemy tries a counter-attack. Speak God's Word and stand for what rightfully belongs to you through Christ and watch God's Word work. Proverbs 18:21 says, *"Death and Life are in the power of the tongue, and those who love it will eat its fruit.*" Psalm 118:17 says, *"I shall not die, but live and declare the works of the Lord."* Psalm 107:20 says, *"He sent His word and healed them, and delivered them from their destruction."* 1 Peter 2:24 says, *"...By whose stripes you were healed."* If the Bible says we were healed, then we are healed. It is finished! We are the healed, just as we are the redeemed! Jesus paid the price for salvation, spirit, soul and body 2,000 years ago (Isaiah 53:3-5, Romans 10:9-10).

(3) HAVING DONE ALL TO STAND

Ephesians 6:13 goes on to say, *"Having done all to stand..."* this is where many lose the battle, especially in the realm of healing. It refers to preparing oneself to stand during negative times. Many are ignorant of God's will concerning healing and health. When difficult times come, they cannot appropriate God's word for their situation and remain sick and continue to struggle. Many Christians do not esteem God's word concerning healing highly, and when sickness attacks they run for answers and try to stand strong. However, without any prior preparation, they ultimately are unable to endure and give up. For example, if a farmer does not plant seed, he will not reap a harvest. The word of God is referred to as seed (Mark 4 and 1 Peter 1:23). If we do not plant the seed of health and healing, how can we expect to reap a harvest of health and healing? This is why I tell Christians not to wait till they are sick and doctors give up hope to find out about divine healing. We need to study and plant the seed now, so we can enjoy a continuous harvest of health and healing in our lives.

The Word of God has life in it, just as a seed has a plant in it. (Hebrews 4:12) The promises in God's word are like seeds. They may seem powerless when they are in the beginning or seed stage, but once you get them inside and keep God's word before you, God's word will rise up and eventually produce powerful results.

Once again, when do we need faith? Lets say I have a physical need in my body. I pray and am healed instantly. Now do I need faith for healing? Absolutely not, as I have already received it. However, if my healing is not manifested immediately, then I need faith to stand for my healing.

Faith in God works when we have not yet received the answer in the physical realm. Faith affects the spiritual realm, bringing to pass our healing. Jesus said in Mark 11:24, *"Therefore I say to you, whatever things you ask when you pray, believe that you receive them, and you will have them."* According to this scripture we receive the thing for which we have prayed the instant we pray for it! Since we are dealing with healing in this book, I will keep my examples to healing. Therefore, we should believe to be healed the instant we pray or are prayed for, whether it is manifested or not. The foundation of faith plays a vital role in standing for healing when it is not immediately manifested.

A good faith test, one the Lord gave me, is to pay attention to how much time we spend thanking and praising Him for His provision, especially during trials. Prayer, thanksgiving and confession of God's word literally stills the attack of the enemy. Jesus said in Matthew 21:6, *"Out of the mouth of babes and nursing infants you have perfected praise."* He was quoting King David in Psalm 8:2, which says, *"Out of the mouth of babes and nursing infants you have ordained strength, because of your enemies, that you may silence the enemy and avenger."* Jesus refers to praise as strength against the enemy.

It is also essential to confess His word after receiving prayer.

Your tongue sets on fire the course of nature (James 3:6). Hebrews 11:1 reads, *"Now faith is the substance* (Greek- realization)
of things hoped for, the evidence (Greek – confidence) *of things not
seen."* Praise to God and confession of His word is an expression
of Faith in God. Faith is the title deed to our prayers being answered. Start praising God for the answer to your prayer.

Galatians 6:9 says, *"Let us not grow weary in while doing good,
for in due season we shall reap if we do not lose heart."* In other
words, we should not lose heart because our breakthrough is on
the way. Jesus broke through for us. He is 'Lord of the Breakthroughs' (2 Samuel 5:20). Keep standing and trusting God's
word! Psalm 30:5 says, *"...weeping may endure for a night, But joy
comes in the morning."* Paul and Silas in the midnight hour ex-
pressed their faith and trust in God by praying and praising God,
and thereafter experienced a tremendous breakthrough (Acts
16:16-34). You might currently be in a midnight hour. Through
it all, praise and thank the Lord for victory. Praise is a weapon
that stills the enemy and drives out depression (Matthew 21:16,
Psalm 8:2, Isaiah 61:3). It also reveals faith in our God and that
we believe that we will receive what we have prayed for and re-
quested.

Satan and his demons do not want to see God's word succeed. In Mark 4:17, Jesus explains the parable where the sower
sows the seed – the word of God. One type of soil, or heart condition, where the Word did not produce fruit was when tribulations and persecution arose for the Word's sake and immediately
they stumbled or became offended. Why? They had no grounding
in the Word, no prior preparation, thus when hard times came,
they were overcome by their circumstances.

(4) STAND THEREFORE

Ephesians 6:14 says, after we have learned and prepared to stand, to keep standing. Therefore stand! Do not give in! Ephesians 6:14-18 tells us the best way to stand is to put on the whole Armor of God. Notice, the sword is the only offensive weapon. The Sword, God's Word, is an offensive and defensive weapon. Interestingly, there is no weapon that provides protection to the back. We are never meant to retreat, regress or give-up! Those who pray in the spirit (tongues- Romans 8:25-28) build their faith. (Jude 20, 1 Corinthians 14:4 & 18). Once we put on the armor, we battle in prayer. When we put on the shield of faith (understand and walk by faith), we will quench all the fiery darts the enemy aims our way.

There have been occasions when I have injured myself, or needed a root canal, etc, and in spite of receiving prayer in faith, the symptoms persisted. I understand God's word regarding healing. I believed I had received, kept confessing it, thanking Jesus for my healing, and in due time God's Word worked as the healing manifested itself.

On one such occasion, I was playing on a city league football team in Kalispell, Montana. While running to catch the ball carrier, a player came running full speed and hit me on my side, damaging my rotator cuff. My arm hung limp and I was unable to move it up without great pain.

I was a single parent doing carpentry work at that time. My two boys, Jesse and Reed, who were quite young at this time, prayed for me. Nothing seemed to happen right away. I believed I received. I went to work the next day and could hardly lift my hammer to frame walls. I kept speaking God's word over my body and thanked the Lord for my healing, even though it was quite painful trying to work. Within two days I was completely healed of the problem and went back to lifting heavy walls and hammering. God will work similarly for anyone who is willing to take the limits off His word and trust Him implicitly. No circumstance or demon can keep God's word from coming to fruition.

Over the years I have met many individuals who had severe physical ailments and were not healed instantly. When there appeared to be no hope, they refused to give up and give place to fear, but walked in faith, trusting Jesus. They built up their most holy faith by praying in the Holy Ghost. As a result, today, many years later, they are walking in divine health.

My mother was one of those who walked in victory over sickness. She was diagnosed with cancer in 1974. She stood in faith for her miracle. Eventually the doctors said they could not understand the mystery that occurred in her blood cells, where there was no trace of cancer. My father and mother used the Word like a pill. She said that everyday she would take her "Gospill." Proverbs 4:22 says, *"For they* (the word) *are life to those that find them, and health* (Hebrew – medicine) *to all their flesh."*

John 14:26, 15:26 and 16:7 refer to the Holy Spirit as our helper or comforter (Greek- also meaning 'standby'). The Holy Spirit keeps us standing strong. All we have to do is acknowledge Him as being our ever-present help in time of trouble. He will always bring us through victoriously. He is in us and standing with us.

CHAPTER 7

RENEWING THE MIND: KEY TO A LASTING CHANGE

I heard this testimony of a man who was afflicted with multiple sclerosis in Glenwood Springs, Colorado. The disease had taken a severe toll on his body confining him to a wheelchair. During that time, his Pastor started teaching on healing and faith. This man sat under the teaching consistently and began to apply what he learned to his circumstances. Within a few months, he was out of the wheelchair, walking with the aid of a cane. A little later, he discarded the cane and could walk a little on his own. As he continued to renew his mind to God's word regarding healing, he was running within a year. This came about as he refused to accept the world's verdict and diagnosis of multiple sclerosis, that he would only deteriorate and there would be no improvement for his condition with the passage of time. Rather than embracing that fact, he choose to embrace God's answer and will for his circumstance and was healed, not instantly, but over the passage of time as he consistently renewed his mind to God's word. That is a perfect example of the power of renewing our mind and doing what God's word says about our circumstances. This can happen to any believer who will have the tenacity to believe and renew their mind to do what God's word says.

WHAT IS TRUE MIND RENEWAL?

In order to witness miracles and healings on a consistent basis renewing the mind to the truth of God's word and who we are in Christ is unprecedented in importance. The concept of renewing the mind can be successfully applied to any area of life, whether for health, holiness, prosperity, marriage, joy, etc.

3 John vs. 2 says, *"Beloved, I pray that you may prosper in all things and be in health, just as your soul prospers."* In this verse, God's desire for us His children is very clear. He desires that we prosper and walk in health. Personally, I adhere to the opinion that we should walk in divine health consistently, rather than constantly being in need of miracle intervention.

As my wife Sharmila and I age, by the grace of God and by standing on His word, we continue to walk in excellent health. Some assume that to walk in health as one ages is impossible. They believe it is only natural for the body to deteriorate with age. Psalms 103:5 says *"Who satisfies your mouth with good things, So that your youth is renewed like the eagle's."* However, as 3 John vs 2 puts it, *"prosperity and health are contingent on our soul."* Our soul prospers as we apply God's word to every aspect of our lives. We can and will prosper in those areas of our lives where we apply God's word. More important than health insurance is the health assurance God's word gives to believers, those knowing who they are in Christ and what they have in Christ.

"I beseech you therefore, brethren, by the mercies of God, that you present your bodies a living sacrifice, holy, acceptable to God, which is your reasonable service. And do not be conformed

to this world, but be transformed by the renewing of your mind, that you may prove what is that good and acceptable and perfect will of God. For I say, through the grace given to me, to everyone who is among you, not to think of himself more highly than he ought to think, but to think soberly, as God has dealt to each person a measure of faith." (Romans 12:1-3)

Verse 2 says not to be conformed (which in Greek means patterned or fashioned to this world or its ways of thinking), but on the contrary, to be transformed by the renewing of your mind. The word transformed here in the Greek means to "go through metamorphosis, to change from one form to another or transfigure."

I do not make this statement. This is God's Word, and it says you and I, and our circumstances can change or be transformed when we renew our mind. What do we renew our mind to? Read on! We renew it to the perfect will of God! God's word is His will (1 John 5:14-15). Also keep in mind Jesus and His Word are the same (John 1:1-4, 14). Jesus and His Word are inseparable. The focus needs to be Jesus and the Word in order to change our circumstances.

1 Corinthians 2:16 says, *"For who has known the mind of the Lord that he may instruct Him? But we have the mind of Christ."* According to this scripture we have the mind of Christ. Walking in the wholeness of the mind of Christ is an everyday task that may take a lifetime. We acquire His mind by diligently studying the Word and applying it to our lives. The more we learn the word of God, the more we have His mind to think, act, and go through life successfully.

Romans 12:2 refers to the *"good and acceptable and perfect will of God"*. When pertaining to healing a number of people are not sure of God's will. How do we know that it is God's will to heal anyone? We know that the Bible is His will and it talks at length on healing. In fact healing was an integral part of Jesus' ministry on earth. We are commanded and commissioned to follow in His footsteps (Mark 16:15-18, John 14:12).

CHANGING THE INSIDE

When one gets saved, what is saved? The spirit! Personally, I do not believe that the body or mind is saved. However, the salvation Jesus purchased for us includes healing for the body and deliverance! James 1:21 says, *"Therefore lay aside all filthiness and overflow of wickedness, and receive with meekness the implanted word, which is able to save your soul."* I believe the soul in this text includes one's mind, will and emotions. For an example, some people are saved, but still struggle with cancer in their physical bodies. In such situations, one needs to renew the mind to the word of God, by studying scripture and applying them to our situation, then our body will come in line with the benefits of the salvation/healing Jesus provided at Calvary.

In spite of being saved, some of us may struggle financially, or battle sickness or demonic torment, even though Christ has redeemed us from all of these. God's word is full of promises for abundant life. If we stand on those promises and apply them to our lives, we will witness a positive change in our circumstances. It is our choice to walk in healing, prosperity, joy etc. God will never force His will on us.

Unfortunately, we live in a society of instant gratification. Stores are stocked with microwaves, fast food restaurants are always busy, individual needs are met instantly. Many pay the price for this kind of mindset. Often in our Christian walk, we desire the principles of instant gratification to apply as well to our finances, health or circumstances. Often our answers do not lie in the instant quick fix but rather they are achieved over a period of time, so that we can mature, learn and something positive is birthed within us for a lifetime. This process comes about as we renew our minds to God's word.

Many are unwilling to go through the steady process of transformation. They want a quick fix. They think that just casting out a demon; popping a pill or blaming others will somehow quickly solve their problems.

When we continually blame outward circumstances on the government, our spouse or children for our problems, but are unwilling to change the inside, we are buying into the enemy's lie that will blind us and bind us and will keep us from lasting change. Renewing our mind, changing the inside, not just the outside will bring about lasting change and freedom. On some occasions, controlling or demonic forces need to be dealt with to bring about change. However, if the mind is not renewed and the inside changed, many end up dealing with the same problem repeatedly (Matthew 12:43-45). If we renew our mind to God's word and live according to the Word, it can bring deliverance and permanent change.

It is unfortunate many embrace a lie that the root of their problem is their spouse, job, or the area one lives in etc. One tends to blame difficulties on external circumstances deceiving oneself. We may move to a different town or change jobs, where for a while life goes on smoothly. Nevertheless, soon the same problems rear their ugly head once again. Why? Because the problems are within us and we brought them with us! For the most part problems will not change unless we make a conscious decision to change by renewing our mind to the word of God.

Romans 12:3 says not to think more highly of ourselves than we ought to think. To truly change, alter or transform our negative situations, we have to understand the need for humility. Many are not humble enough to acknowledge the need for change and thus continue to be beaten up by their sickness, poverty, depression, discouragements, marital problems, etc. Many do not take evaluations that cause them to acknowledge their need for change. Pride stands in their way of making a lasting change.

There have been times in my life where I had to acknowledge that my thoughts and actions were not in line with God's word. I had to humble myself, repent and do what the Word said to change my negative circumstances.

I have noticed many Charismatic and Pentecostal churches believe in divine healing, but see very few, if any, healings. Why is that? First, there is no foundation laid on the subject of renewing the mind. Therefore, no transformation takes place in the physical bodies of those needing healing or deliverance. Secondly, true mind renewal is not just mental ascent to a truth in God's Word. It is in your doing what you believe that brings about the true and lasting change. It starts by changing the inside!

Renewing our mind to what God's Word says will take us down a road to victory. It all comes down to our willingness to allow the Word to change our outlook in life. We need to be examples of the Gospel working powerfully and transforming our lives. The Gospel is loaded with the good news that Jesus has come to heal, forgive, bless and deliver. We can walk in all these things on a consistent basis.

Romans 10:17 says, *"So then faith comes by hearing, and hearing by the word of God."* Faith comes by the hearing God's word, then acting upon God's word. Faith is what activates God's miracle working power! Faith based upon renewing our mind to what God's word says transforms our circumstances.

Many times to bring about change in our thought life and circumstances, we need to be open to learning from others. Some are unwilling to go outside of the belief system of those with whom they fellowship. As a result, things never change. Some have the knowledge of what to do for their circumstances but never act on what the Word says. 1 Corinthians 8:1 says *"We know that we all have knowledge. Knowledge puffs up, but love edifies."* Just having a knowledge of God's word without any practical experience has led some down a road of pride and arrogance. They have no power to change their lives for the better. It is a lot like the leaven that Jesus described. It inflates, but offers no nutritional value. Change and transformation comes when we do God's Word.

GOD'S THOUGHTS VS OUR THOUGHTS

Let the wicked forsake his way, and the unrighteous man his thoughts: and let him return unto the Lord, and He will have mercy on him; and to our God, for He will abundantly pardon. For my thoughts are not your thoughts, neither are your ways my ways, saith the Lord. For as the heavens are higher than the earth, so are my ways higher than your ways, and my thoughts than your thoughts. For as the rain comes down, and the snow from heaven and do not return there, but water the earth, and make it bring forth and bud, that it may give seed to the sower and bread to the eater, so shall My word be that goes forth from My mouth; it shall not return to Me void, but it shall accomplish what I please, and it shall prosper in the thing for which I sent it. (Isaiah 55:7-11).

Just how far are the heavens above the earth? The heavens are much higher than the earth. That might give you somewhat of an idea of how much higher God's thoughts and ways are compared to our thoughts and ways.

The above scriptures emphasize abandoning our old way of life with its thoughts once we come to Christ. Why? Because God's ways and thoughts are much higher and superior to man's! Our ways and thoughts are usually influenced by our upbringing. If we have been without the word of God, then in all likelihood our lifestyle and thoughts will not be conducive to producing positive results in our lives.

God says, "For My thoughts are not your thoughts, neither are your ways my ways..." How are we to successfully change our ways and thoughts to align with His? By studying His word, as His thoughts and ways that are found in the word. This should make every Christian extremely hungry for the word of God.

How are we going to witness miracles of Biblical proportions – the blind seeing, the deaf hearing, the dead resurrected etc.? By tapping into the power of His Word and thinking like He does. So much of what is taught in Christian circles today is just natural thinking that does not include the supernatural power of God. All it does is help Christians to cope, but never to walk in the supernatural power of God or to live in victory over their circumstances. We need to go beyond that kind of thinking and tap into God's thoughts and ways.

I am absolutely convinced that the Word of God has the power and ability to change – spiritually, mentally, financially and physically - any negative circumstance to a positive one. If we call upon and use the Word of God it does not return void, but as it says in the above scripture, "...*it* (the word) *shall not return to Me void, but it shall accomplish what I please, and it shall prosper* (Hebrew- succeed in its fulfillment) *in the thing for which I sent it*" (Isaiah 55:11).

If God says that something is ours, whether it is joy, healing, peace, prosperity etc. then it is ours. But how do we appropriate it? We renew our mind to His Word. It will change our circumstances because His Word has the power to do so, to literally transform us or our circumstances.

I was ministering on the Blood Indian Reserve in Alberta, Canada years ago, where a woman was healed of a hernia without anyone laying hands on her. I called out her condition as a word of knowledge and later she testified that she felt an invisible hand push the hernia back into her body. Within a month and a half, she also lost 50 pounds.

About two years later, I returned to the same Reserve and ministered in a healing service. I shared with them the woman's testimony from two years earlier. A charismatic catholic woman in the congregation felt that God was speaking to her through the testimony. She appropriated it for herself and was healed of a hernia while sitting in her chair. She was healed as she heard God's Word regarding her physical situation, before we even started ministering to those needing healing. That is the power behind God's word and sharing testimonies of His power and love.

How do we renew our minds? It is like planting seed. It starts with a thought. The thought becomes an action. The action becomes a habit. The habit becomes a lifestyle and the lifestyle becomes a stronghold. We can have positive or negative strongholds in our lives, depending on how we were raised and what we are being taught right now. We need to build on the positive things in our lives and tear down the negative strongholds in our minds and hearts.

2 Corinthians 10:4-5 says *"For the weapons of our warfare are not carnal but mighty in God for pulling down strongholds, casting down arguments and every high thing that exalts itself against the knowledge of God, bringing every thought into captivity to the obedience of Christ."* Our mind is where the battle takes place!

Jesus said Mark 4:17 says, *"and they have no root in themselves, and so endure only for a time. Afterward, when tribulation or persecution arises for the word's sake, immediately they stumble."* Jesus is referring to people with no or little roots in the Word of God. They quickly received the Word, but the results were temporary. As they had no or little roots, when trials and persecution arose for the Word's sake and they immediately fell. The way we wage war with an enemy that Jesus already defeated is with the truth of God's word. That is how we enforce his defeat and walk in all that Christ provided for us 2,000 years ago.

Satan and his demons' plan is not to allow the Word to work in your life. That is why Jesus said *"persecution arises for the word's sake"* (Mark 4:17). They know the only way they can defeat Christians is when they do not apply God's Word to their circumstances. This battle we fight with the enemy of our soul all comes down to what we do with the truth of God's Word. Do we apply it and experience it or do we listen to demonic lies that will bind us and blind us to the truth (God's Word) that can set us free?

Many believers are feeling disoriented. They run and base their life on their experiences, good or bad. They are unstable emotionally. One bad thing that can come out of this is building a belief system on negative experiences. We need to base our life on the word of God and get our experiences to line up with God's word. We cannot build our belief system on negative experiences. This is where false doctrine comes in and where many believers live lives of defeat. This is why it is important to renew our minds to God's Word. Luke 1:37 (amp) says, *"For with God nothing is ever impossible and no word from God shall be without power or impossible of fulfillment."*

If believers really understood the power of God's Word to transform us, we would see lasting change in our lives. We would get our roots down deep in the Word and not be shaken by anything the enemy throws our way. Jesus said *"Therefore whoever hears these sayings of Mine, and does them, I will liken him to a wise man who built his house on the rock: and the rain descended, the floods came, and the winds blew and beat on that house; and it did not fall, for it was founded on the rock"* (Matthew 7:26-27).

EXAMPLES OF GOD'S THOUGHTS VS. THE WORLD'S THOUGHTS

Let us look at examples of the world's thoughts vs. God's thoughts. According to Romans 12:2, we need to remember that we do not have to be fashioned and patterned after the world and that we can change our circumstances when we apply God's Word.

The world says, "its flu season: you are going to get it. Get your medicine chest stocked with anti-flu medication, allergy medication etc." Once during the supposed flu season, a gentleman greeted me with, "the flu is going around; you are going to get it." I did not receive his confession, but I awoke the following morning with the flu. During those days, I was starting to learn and understand faith. I started confessing God's Word of healing over myself, as I parked cars in downtown Minneapolis, Minnesota in 30 degree below zero weather. My office was a little shack that could not keep the cold out. I listened to tapes on healing by Kenneth Copeland and listened to radio preachers sharing on Christ the Healer. Within two hours, I was completely healed. Then when people said the flu was going around, I would say "Yes and praise God it is going way around me. It is not coming near me."

The opposite of the world's view on sickness, the Word of God says to lay hands on the sick and they shall recover (Mark 16:17-18). By the stripes of Jesus we are healed (Isaiah 53:4-5, 1 Peter 2:24). God's Word will be life unto those that find it, and health (Hebrew-medicine) to all their flesh (Proverbs 4:22).

The world says one has every right to be depressed and have self-pity when everything is going awry. One can also accept the world's diagnosis that one has to live in depression because of chemical imbalances, using medication throughout life. On the contrary, one can rise up with the Word of God, which says regarding depression in Nehemiah 8:10, *"the joy of the Lord is our strength"*, and to *"put on the garment of praise for the spirit of heaviness"* or depression (Isaiah 61:13). Joy and praise can turn around one's circumstances and give strength to rise out of those circumstances.

James 1:2, *"My brethren, count it all joy when you fall into various trials"* (in the Greek means tests and temptations). The best way to break out of negative circumstances is to rejoice and praise the Lord. Joy is part of the fruit of the Spirit. It should automatically flow from within us, regardless of our circumstances, because of the nature of Christ within us. A fruit tree does not have to struggle to produce fruit, because the fruit is the outcome of what is within the tree; similarly as Christians we should not struggle with operating in joy, the fruit of the Spirit is within us.

1 Thessalonians 5:18 says, *"in everything* (Greek- every way, every manner, every place) *give thanks for this is the will of God in Christ Jesus concerning you."* This is not implying that we thank God for our trials and tribulations, rather we thank Him through them. This way we walk in victory! I believe that joy and praise are powerful weapons that can pull us through or out of the worst situations that may confront us during our lives. If Satan and his demons cannot steal your joy, then they can not steal your goods.

Jeremiah 15:16 in the Amplified version reads, *"Your words were found, and I ate them, and Your word was to me the joy and the rejoicing of my heart."* I had a puppy named Roscoe who once ate my pocket size Amplified Bible. Thereafter he remained very happy, even after I yelled at him for eating my Bible. Eating the Word really brought joy to his life.

Can you see a pattern here? The world thinks one way. In fact, many Christians are given to thinking as the world does because they have not heeded the need to renew the mind to God's thoughts and ways. As Christians, we can and should think at a higher level, which can only happen as we renew our minds and think God's thoughts.

But the path of the just is like the shining sun, That shines even brighter unto the perfect day. The way of the wicked is like darkness; They do not know what makes them stumble. My son, give attention to my words; Incline your ears to my sayings. Do not let them depart from your eyes; Keep them in the midst of your heart; For they are life to those that find them, And health to all their flesh. Keep your heart with all diligence, For out of it spring the issues of life. (Proverb 4:18-23).

According to verse 18, the closer we get to the return of Jesus Christ, the brighter our path gets. What makes our path brighter? Psalms 119:105 says, *"Your word is a lamp to my feet And a light to my path."* Psalm 119:130 says, *"The entrance of your words gives light; It gives understanding to the simple."* According to these scriptures what is lighting our path? His Word is lighting our path, which will bring about more revelation, more miracles, signs and wonders! The wicked stumble because they do not have positive solutions for their situations. They do not walk in the light of the Word.

Proverbs 4:21 says, *"Do not let them* (God's Words) *depart from your eyes; Keep them in the midst of your heart."* Do we as Christians really adhere to this truth? Some people complain that they received prayer for healing once, but healing was not manifested, hence they do not believe it is God's will to heal. If we are truly keeping God's Word in our heart then it will lead to a transformation of the physical circumstances.

Unfortunately, there are some people I should not even pray for, as I know that they do not desire to change their lifestyle and deal with issues that brought about the sickness or problems initially. What will prayer avail if individuals that know better refuse to renew their mind to the Word of God and change the very thing that opened the door to problems, sickness or demons? At the most, it is a temporary cure! Sometimes the Lord will have me tell a person to press into something specific in the Word of

God for permanent change, healing and deliverance.

Proverbs 4:22 says, *"For they* (God's Word) a*re life to those who find them, And health* (Hebrew-medicine) *to all their flesh."* The Word of God is medicine to our flesh.

Proverbs 4:23 says *"Keep your heart with all diligence, For out of it spring the issues of life."* Many miss it in this area, as they do not keep their heart with all diligence. What if I chose not to clean my house, do the dishes, laundry etc. on a regular basis? Soon I will have a dirty unkempt home. The same analogy can be applied to our (spiritual) heart. If we chose to neglect our hearts, not tending to it, then it will gravitate towards evil, sickness, bondage and defeat. In Mark 7:15 Jesus says, *"There is nothing that enters a man from outside which can defile him; but the things which come out of him, those are the things that defile a man."*

Jesus said, *"Either make the tree good and its fruit good, or else make the tree bad and its fruit bad; for a tree is known by its fruit. Brood of vipers! How can you, being evil, speak good things? For out of the abundance of the heart the mouth speaks. A good man out of the good treasure of his heart brings forth good things, and an evil man out of the evil treasure brings forth evil things. But I say to you that for every idle word men may speak, they will give account of it in the day of Judgment. For by your words you will be justified, and by your words you will be condemned"* (Matthew 12:33-37).

A tree will only produce what is within it. It is the same with our heart or belief system! In terms of healing, if a person is constantly afflicted with sickness and disease, then there is a good chance sickness is in the person's heart. The principle applies to poverty, depression, victory, health, joy, etc. Some Christians say they believe one way, but continually experience the opposite.

For the most part you will only live out what it is in your heart (what you really believe), whether good or bad. If you do not like what you are experiencing in life on a continual basis then begin to renew your mind to what God's Word says about your circumstances and let His Word transform any negative circumstances in your life. Simply have the tenacity to believe what He says in His Word is true and apply it in your life, and you will experience His word at work for you eventually.

What is the foremost thing we hear every day? It is our own words, our own voice! Jesus cautioned us to take heed to what we hear, for with the measure we hear, it will be measured back to us (Mark 4:24). Jesus said *"...For out of the abundance of the heart the mouth speaks"* (Matthew 12:34). What is inside your heart will be spoken out, whether sickness, victory, defeat or prosperity. What is in your heart is your future. If we do not like what we see and hear then we need to change.

Proverbs 23:7 says, *"For as he thinks in his heart, so is he..."*. In other words, we are what we think. Many desire to know what the future holds. Each one of us can know what is in our future. All we have to do is to take a deep look into our hearts. What picture is within us? That is what we are going to live each day. If we do not like what is within us, then we can change it by renewing our mind to the word of God. Once again, Jesus said in verse 34 *"For out of the abundance of the heart the mouth speaks."* We can tell what is in the heart by what comes out of the mouth, especially when our circumstances do not look good.

PUTTING OFF AND PUTTING ON

If indeed you have heard Him and have been taught by Him, as the truth is in Jesus: That you put off' concerning your former conduct, the old man which grows corrupt according to the deceitful lusts, and be renewed in the spirit of your mind, and that you put on the new man which was created according to God, in true righteousness and holiness (Ephesians 4:21-24).

In these scriptures, we see three essential actions to renew the mind. Firstly, putting off, secondly, renewed in the spirit of our mind and thirdly, putting on.

Often we are guilty of the willingness to put on, without putting off, i.e. dealing with the old self with its thoughts and habits, and soon enough, problems arise. Would it not be ridiculous that when a baby needs a diaper change, instead of changing the diaper, one just puts on a clean one over the messy dirty one? What happens? In a while there is a bigger mess to clean up than previously. Similarly renewing the mind is not merely adopting new thought patterns, but also entails completely giving up old ways of thinking that are detrimental to positive living. It is being renewed in the spirit of our mind, that will change our negative circumstances (which in the Greek is the principal part of our mind).

Every individual grows up with certain strongholds, negative or positive, that tend to govern that person's reactions to circumstances in life. These are stored in the subconscious or spirit of your mind and manifest themselves in our reactions during various situations in life. When I would go through hard times, I would indulge in self-pity. Until I realized that I had to break this pattern of behavior and renew my mind to God's Word when trials came, responding in joy, which I have since done. With that attitude, I now walk in victory over those circumstances that used to beat me up.

ISRAEL – AN EXAMPLE TO US

The children of Israel are a prime example of an entire generation that chose not to put off the old way of thinking. They wandered aimlessly for 40 years, despite the fact that God had promised them possession of the Promised Land. The entire generation, except Joshua and Caleb, had to pass away before the Israelites could take possession of the Promised Land. Why did this happen? Did God turn back on His promise? No! It was the disobedience, the negative mind set and confession of the people that kept them in bondage. They had grown up in bondage as slaves in Egypt. God supernaturally delivered them from Egypt. Now it was their responsibility to renew their minds to God's promises, get rid of the slave mindset, believe in what God said they could do and possess the Promised Land, which they failed in doing. It is our job as believers to renew our minds to what God says about us and who we are in Christ.

To understand this better, let me quote from my book *You Can Tap into Christ's Healing Power* once again (chapter 5 The Power of Confessing God's Word). "Referring to the children of Israel 1 Corinthians 10:11 says, *"Now all these things happened to them as examples, and they were written for our admonition, upon whom the end of ages have come."* God brought them out of Egypt with powerful signs and wonders. He told them He would lead them into the Promised Land. Most of the Israelites never made it there because the image they had within was negative and full of unbelief, which manifested itself in their constant grumbling and complaining.

As they stood on the edge of the Promised Land after sending out twelve spies, who saw how good the land was, most of them then gave into unbelief and complaining. Many times when one sees the critical spirit and complaining, unbelief and offense are working hand in hand. Judging, complaining, offense and unbelief all work hand in hand to prevent the anointing of God from flowing. These attitudes will keep the miracle working power of God from working in one's life.

Numbers 13:30-33 reads, *"Then Caleb quieted the people before Moses, and said, 'Let us go up at once and take possession, for we are well able to overcome it.' But the men who had gone up with him said, 'we are not able to go up against the people, for they are stronger than we.' And they gave the children of Israel a bad report of the land which they had spied out...' There we saw the giants... and we were like grasshoppers in our own sight, and so we were in their sight."* Verse 32 clearly states the negative report given by the ten spies on the land. It was a report steeped in unbelief. Notice their self image; it had not changed since coming out of Egypt even though God had performed so many signs and wonders in their midst. They said, *"we were like grasshoppers in our own sight and so we were in their sight."* This was not God's impression of His people. They had forgotten one very important thing, the God who brought them out of Egypt! Romans 8:31 says *"...If God is for us, who can be against us?"*

After giving the negative report, Numbers 14:11 gives an insight into the Lord's anger with their continual unbelief and complaining. *"Then the Lord said to Moses: How long will these people reject Me? And how long will they not believe Me, with all the signs which I performed among them."* How were they rejecting God? By simply not trusting in Him! Hebrews 11:6 says, *"But without faith it is impossible to please Him, for he who comes to God must believe that He is, and that He is a rewarder of those who diligently seek Him."* Even today this dilemma persists. God is performing miracles all over the world, yet many Christians refuse to trust God and walk by faith in His Word. Many will mock those who take God at His Word and confess it.

40 years after this negative report of unbelief, Joshua and Caleb led the next generation into the Promised Land. It is interesting to note what Rahab shares with the next set of spies as to what the people of that land thought of Israel and their God in Joshua 2:9-11: *"and [Rahab] said to the men: 'I know that the Lord has given you the land, that the terror of you has fallen on us, and that all the inhabitants of the land are fainthearted because of you. For we heard how the Lord dried up the water of the Red Sea for you when you came out of Egypt, and what you did to the kings of the Amorites who were on the other side of the Jordan, Sihon and Og, whom you utterly destroyed. And as soon as we heard these things, our hearts melted; neither did there remain any more courage in anyone because of you, for the Lord your God, He is God in heaven above and on earth beneath."*

When did the inhabitants of Jericho become fainthearted, with melting hearts and no strength or courage left in them? When they heard what God did to Egypt when Israel was preparing to possess the Promised Land 40 years earlier. It was their unbelief and negative confession that kept them from entering into the Promised Land. They could have easily conquered the Promised Land, but their negative image and confession stopped them from entering in. There are many Christians God has wanted to bless or meet their needs but a negative self image and confession has short-circuited the power of God from moving on behalf of their need.

When Joshua who had been around the unbelieving spies,

prepared to march around Jericho, it is almost humorous to see what he does in Joshua 6:10. *"Now Joshua had commanded the people, saying, You shall not shout or make any noise with your voice, nor shall a word proceed out of your mouth, until the day I say to you, Shout! Then you shall shout."* To paraphrase what he said, 'this time keep your mouths shut'. I tend to believe that many who marched around Jericho wanted to complain of the stupidity of the mission, that it would not work. Instead, Joshua commanded them to be quiet until he gave the order to shout. Jericho was a huge fortified city. On the city walls they raced chariots. When they finally shouted, this huge fortified city fell to the ground. Only Rahab's home was left standing.

One can speak negatively, complain and remain, or can start to praise God, confess His Word, which is confessing His faithfulness and watch His mighty power at work to meet whatever need one may have."

TRANSFORMED INTO CHRIST'S IMAGE

I like the way 2 Corinthians 3:17-18 reads in the Amplified version, *"Now the Lord is the Spirit, and where the Spirit of the Lord is, there is liberty – emancipation from bondage, freedom. And all of us, as with unveiled face (because we) continue to behold* (in the word of God*) as in a mirror the glory of the Lord, are constantly being transfigured into His very own image in ever increasing splendor and from one degree of glory to another,* (for this comes) *from the Lord (Who is) the Spirit."*

I particularly like how it says that as we behold the Word of God, we will be transformed into Christ's very own image. This is exactly what I did on my first trip to India in 1986, where I conducted a citywide, open-air campaign. In the months prior to my trip I began meditating on Christ the Healer. I read books on healing and became one with the vision of Christ the Healer. I was constantly confessing that I would see the blind healed, even though my only exposure to the same was in the Bible and on a Reinhardt Bonkke video. One of my friends questioned my belief of seeing blind eyes opened. He asked me what made me think I would see blind eyes opened (because I had never had up to that time). I said, because "I am going over to India knowing who I am in Christ and He will do the work through me and He will be opening blind eyes."

Once in India, I spent hours studying healing and in intercession, praying in tongues. I was in a place of complete dependence on the Lord. Initially, whatever could go wrong in campaign did. There were two interpreters fist fighting to interpret for me. The first two nights of the campaign after I gave the salvation call, before I prayed for the sick, one Pastor would request to pray. He would pray in Teligu and dismiss the people, as he did not believe in healing. The third night I caught on to what he was doing and did not let him pray. That night I asked the people to bring up anyone who was completely blind, so I could pray and demonstrate Christ's power and compassion to heal as proof that Jesus was alive. A senior lady who had been blind for 20 years came up. After receiving prayer she could not see instantly, but within a few minutes as she praised the Lord for restoring her sight, saw a vision of the Bible and her eyes opened. Since that day we have seen 100's of individuals testify of sight being restored to them in our campaigns.

How did I get to this place of seeing miracles signs and wonders? Did I have an angelic visitation or did Jesus appear to me? The answer is an unequivocal no! I merely started to renew my mind to the Word of God regarding healing. By doing so, I was transformed into the image of Christ the Healer.

Whatever you desire to see – Jesus the lover, the forgiver, the soul winner, etc- start beholding it in His Word and you and your circumstances will be transformed. Start believing in the power and integrity of His Word. Act on it. Live it. You will experience it. You will see miracles and transformation take place.

CHAPTER 8

HOW JESSE ANDERSON OVERCAME HIS ROADBLOCK TO HEALING

I share this testimony of my son Jesse's healing of cancer with his permission. I was a single father raising two boys from 1989 until May 20, 1995, when I married Sharmila. After I married Sharmila, Jesse, my older son, went back and forth between living with us and his mother and stepfather. He spent more time with them, but the relationship he had with his mother and stepfather was not good. Jesse was struggling in different areas of his life. While living with us in 1999, I had to make a difficult decision after many warnings to Jesse, to send him back to his mother. I could not minster to Jesse at that time or be relevant to him, in regard to the course his life was taking. All I could do was love him and pray for him.

Jesse became very angry with me for being what he perceived as too strict and for sending him back to live with his mother. He felt rejected. He also did not like that I was gone on short term missions trips (a week to three weeks at a time) a few times a year. He was also very angry with his mother and his stepfather for their lifestyle.

Jesse began to get heavily involved with hardcore drugs and alcohol and drifted away from Jesus. Jesse himself says that he chose that lifestyle because, by doing so, he fit in with his peers and felt accepted. His friends did not force drugs or alcohol on him, but he willingly chose that lifestyle. As tension grew with his mother and stepfather, Jesse moved out to be on his own with a close friend in Connecticut.

During July 2002, at 18 years old, Jesse became very sick. He contacted a cold that he was unable to recover from; severe bruising and extreme fatigue set in. Jesse thought it was because of his constant partying. He checked with some doctors and they ran some tests. At that time, Jesse emailed his mother, whom he had not spoken to in four months and told her he was very sick. Shortly after, he began sleeping for 23 hours a day, unable to eat anything.

His mother came and took him to a doctor in Vermont, where she was living. The doctor did a blood test and within a few hours had diagnosed him with Acute Myloid Leukemia. Jesse was hospitalized immediately in the Burlington, Vermont hospital. The doctor told them that if he had not come in when he did, he would have been dead within days.

Jesse's mother immediately contacted me with the bad news, not knowing whether Jesse would live or die. Upon receiving the phone call and hearing the news, the Holy Spirit immediately quickened Psalms 112:7 to me. It says, *"He will not be afraid of evil tidings; His heart is steadfast, trusting in the Lord."* That night, Sharmila had a very vivid dream of Jesse exchanging the blood of Jesus for worldly (filthy) blood. Sharmila and I were on a ministry trip heading out east at that time and continued on to Vermont to see Jesse.

As Sharmila and I prayed for Jesse, we felt that we were dealing with a spiritual root that caused his sickness. We felt strongly that, once he was able to deal with this root and receive the blood of Jesus back in his life, he would be miraculously healed. The book *A More Excellent Way* by Henry W. Wright deals with spiritual roots to disease. It says many times leukemia can be caused by deep rooted bitterness caused by unresolved rejection or feelings of rejection between a father and child. This in turn causes a breach in a relationship.

Jesse told me that when he was admitted to the hospital, the paperwork had a section asking his religious affiliations. Jesse marked down that he did not believe in God and remembered thinking to himself that he truly did not believe Jesus was the Son of God. Jesse did not even care if he lived or died.

The same day that Jesse was admitted into the hospital, the doctors began heavy doses of chemotherapy. He was in much pain and suffered constant nausea; gangrene had set in on his left shin. While we were there, the doctors wanted to perform a skin graft because of the severity of the gangrene. Jesse let us pray over him. Right after that, the doctor came in to make the call whether to do the skin graft or not. He looked at the shin as it was improving after prayer and decided against the graft.

When Sharmila and I arrived in Burlington, we began to pray for him and minister Christ's healing power. I remember bringing him a CD of Delirious, one of his favorite worship groups earlier in his life. One song he was very drawn to listen to at that time was "Find me at the River." Some of the lyrics go: *"find me at the river... find me on my knees with my soul laid bare. Even though you're gone and I'm cracked and dry find me at the river. I am waiting here."*

In December 2002, while between chemo sessions, Jesse was released from the hospital. One night, he went out to a movie. He ended up catching pneumonia and ran a fever of 104. Because of the chemo, his immune system was greatly compromised and it became a very serious threat to his life. The doctors admitted him into the ICU and put him into a drug induced coma. He was given 128 milligrams of Ativan per day to keep him under. An average of 4 milligrams of Ativan per day is used to help people with anxiety attacks to calm them down. Jesse was in this drug induced coma for 10 days.

The doctors did not know if he would live or die. We had been given Psalms 118:17 as a verse to hold on to during this time. It says, *"I shall not die, but live, And declare the works of the Lord."* One of our prayer partners, Patti, reminded me of that verse as I left to catch a medical emergency flight to be with Jesse. It was amazing; during that entire time by Jesse's bedside, I had a supernatural joy. The doctor said, "we do not know if he will make it through the night." I told him, "Jesse will make it." I read the Gospel of Mark to Jesse and prayed in his room. I can say it was very peaceful; he never once talked back to me.

Jesse dreamt while in the coma. He said he felt like he was in a prison and the chains of his decisions – the drugs, the drinking, the stealing, the lying - were holding him down in darkness. Then he dreamt that he was weightless, free of the chains, like Jesus was cleansing of him of his past. When he came out of the coma, a minister was in the room, and he began to talk to Jesse about Jesus. He describes that time as a spiritual awakening for him. He believed in God, but he did not invite Christ back into to his life at that time.

The cancer went into remission and Jesse moved back to Connecticut. By the spring of 2003, Jesse fell back into his partying lifestyle. Only this time he did not enjoy it like he had in the past. He began questioning why he was doing it. As he began drawing closer to Christ, in April he cast out a prayer to God. He said "If you are real, show yourself to me." Little did he know how his heavenly Father would take him up on that prayer the very next month.

While at a party doing drugs, he heard an audible voice say, "You cannot leave me." He had heard those exact words in a rock song he listened to. He knew it was a demon speaking to him. He was very frightened by the voice. He walked outside and got into his car and began praying. His asked, "God make me sober." Instantly he sobered up. Then he repented to Christ. The Holy Spirit began guiding him on what demons to cast out. One of the first demons he cast out was fear. When he commanded it to go, everything turned black and he was very frightened. He commanded the demon to go by the blood of Jesus and it left. One by one he cast out demons: addiction, pride and more. When he commanded sickness to go, he said, "in Jesus' name, sickness be gone by the blood of Jesus." Immediately, he felt a sensation, like his blood began to bubble, he could see the blood in his veins was green under his skin. As Jesus began to cleanse his blood, the color of his skin, which had been very pale, changed to a very healthy color.

The last demon he cast out was pride. After he cast out pride, he saw a group of his party buddies standing outside the car wondering what was going on with him. He rolled down the window and said to his friends, "I'm OK! I accepted Jesus." He left that lifestyle behind.

For the next week, all he did was pray and read the Bible. The Holy Spirit showed him how He had a plan for his life and would bring the woman of his dreams into his life and make him successful. Jeremiah 29:11- 13 says, *"For I know the thoughts that I think toward you, says the LORD, thoughts of peace and not of evil, to give you a future and a hope. Then you will call upon Me and go and pray to Me, and I will listen to you. And you will seek Me and find Me, when you search for Me with all your heart."*

Shortly after this encounter, he called me. He told me how nothing I had said had related to him earlier, but now he could understand and wanted to serve Jesus. Exactly one year after he was in that drug-induced coma, he began attending World Impact Bible Institute in St. Catharines, Ontario, Canada. In the past seven years, he has joined me on mission trips to Peru, India and Nepal.

Today, Jesse is happily married to Melanie, whom he met while in Bible School in Canada. They currently have two children. Ever since dealing with the roadblocks to his healing and the spiritual roots in his life that attracted leukemia, he has been cancer free and walking in health. I am so grateful, with tears in my eyes at times, thinking how Jesus has set him free, blessed him and restored our relationship. Today, Jesse and I have a good relationship. As a father, I am very proud of my son and where God has brought him.

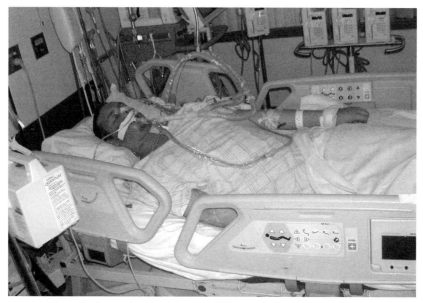

My son, Jesse Anderson, in a coma and on life support. Burlington, Vermont– January 2003.

One year later, preaching at Bible School completely freed of Leukemia! Leukemia free to this day!

CHAPTER 9

HOW SARAH NICHOLSON OVERCAME HER ROADBLOCK TO HEALING

In Sarah's words: "More than ten years ago, I went through a period of unexplainable suffering, an intense time of testing and spiritual growth. My sickness came suddenly. One day, some sort of lumps began forming on my left rib cage, under the skin. It felt very sore and soon spread to cover much of my rib cage, armpits, hips and groin. It seemed that there were new lumps every day. It was very tender and my abdomen was swollen. Eventually, my entire lymphatic system had lumps. I even had difficulty swallowing food, as the growths were filling my throat.

Deciding what to do about the growths became a stark reality as I watched the symptoms grow steadily worse. I went to my family doctor. He thought that the growths were some sort of scar tissue in my muscles, though I tried to convince him that they had just shown up. He scheduled my next appointment with another doctor, who specialized in internal medicine. All this time, I was recalling how quickly my Dad's body had filled with tumors, followed by his death ten days later with cancer.

I was troubled by the uncertainty I felt and the possibility of dying. I had four young children under ten years old at the time. Each night, after they fell asleep, I would go into their rooms and cry out to God, praying for the ability to live and see them raised for God's glory. My husband was so busy with his responsibilities being self-employed that he could not do much to help me besides giving encouragement and praying with me for healing. I struggled in my prayers for healing because I didn't know if it was really God's will for me to be healed. I reasoned in my heart that perhaps I could bring greater glory to God's name by dying young, like the martyrs. The question remained how could I know for sure what God's will was for my life? The answers that I got from questions like this were varied. It seemed that everyone had an opinion about what was God's will and I found that talking about the problem seemed to make it worse and more confusing.

The ability of the medical world to cure me was questionable. I had seen how quickly my Dad died after the doctors had biopsied his tumors. It seemed to open the tumors and spread them. So at each of my doctor appointments, I would pray that God would direct the physicians to just advise me and pass me on to the next caregiver, without suggesting biopsies. This is what happened at each visit. After several exams, I realized that the medical world could do nothing more for me without their traditional methods and I withdrew from this path to search for alternatives. I did not want to spend a lot of time and money on a system that I was not convinced could help me.

This decision unleashed a whole new series of challenges. Well-meaning friends and family often exhorted me to get medical aid. They even accused me of not loving my family because they thought that I had given up on any "real" help. But I was convinced that God was God and He was also the Great Physician. I knew that He was able to heal me. It just sounded a little odd to people when I tried to explain it to them. I had seen God work in other situations in my life in incredible ways so I knew that He was powerful, but was He willing? How could I know for sure?

As time went on, while I was searching the Scriptures for a solution, I was still pursuing help from other people. I had people praying for me around the world. Healing prayer meetings were held at two different churches for me and I tried special elimination diets to ease the stress on my body. I even had a strange woman call me from Texas to tell me that she had muscle-tested me over the phone, though I had never spoken to her before. Though I felt desperate to feel better, I didn't have peace about her approach. I had an even stronger desire to know what God's will was for my life.

I really believed that God could heal me without all of these other influences and I desired to be obedient to the Scripture, so I asked the pastor and elders of our church to anoint me with oil and to pray the prayer of faith that is mentioned in James 5:14-15, which says, *"Is anyone among you sick? Let him call for the elders of the church, and let them pray over him, anointing him with oil in the name of the Lord. And the prayer of faith will save the sick, and the Lord will raise him up. And if he has committed sins, he will be forgiven."* We met after church in a little room and the pastor proceeded to warn me that he did not want me to lose my faith if God did not heal me. He said that we could ask God to heal, but cannot know His will on this matter. He also told me the story of a man whose wife was paralyzed and dying, who demanded that his wife live. He said that God answered his prayer and the man's wife lived, but was a human vegetable the rest of her life. This warning that I might get something bad from God was discouraging to me. The elders then prayed for me, but did not have oil to anoint me. I did not feel that any of the elders had much faith when they prayed. I testified to them, before I left, that the only reason that I had them pray was out of obedience to the scripture in James and exhorted them that they should have more faith, be obedient to God's word, and that I still believed that God would heal me.

To clear up the issue about whether God would give you a bad gift when you ask for something good is simply answered in the scripture in Luke 11:11-13: *"If a son shall ask bread of any of you that is a father, will he give him a stone? Or if he ask a fish, will he give him a serpent? Or if he ask an egg, will he offer him a scorpion? If you then, being evil, know how to give good gifts to your children; how much more shall your heavenly Father give the Holy Spirit to them that ask him?"*

I found a source of hope attending a local cowboy church every Friday night. Brent Baumann, the pastor, would encourage me to believe God for healing by telling me that it was not God's will for a mother of four young children to die. I couldn't understand how he was so confident about knowing what God's will was for me. He was very convincing on this matter and would not budge, though I peppered him with all the arguments that I had heard from others. This caused our family to really search to find what God's will would be for my life. How could God's ministers believe such opposite things in regard to healing?

Each week, at the meetings, different faith teachers would come to preach messages that totally stretched my understanding. I felt drawn to continue to listen. They gave strong words about the Lord and healing. They prayed with authority and certainty that their prayers would be answered. After the meetings, I would go forward to receive the prayer ministry. Many of the speakers would pray against a spirit of infirmity. I would go home, hopeful that I would see a difference in the lumps. Disappointed because I didn't see any visible difference, I even felt that the symptoms got worse. I realized later that I was not "holding fast" to the profession of my faith (Hebrews 10:2). I was still looking at the symptoms and speaking doubtful words about the faith and words of the preachers.

The turning point for me actually came very quietly, through a Scripture that I found written by King David when he asked the question in Psalm 88:10-11a; *"Shall the dead arise and praise you (God)? Selah. Shall your lovingkindness be declared in the grave?"* The obvious answer to this question was that it was not possible to praise God from the grave, but that one must be alive to be able to worship God. This seems like an unlikely healing Scripture, but with it I finally put the question to rest about whether it was God's will for me to live. The issue was settled for me in my heart. From this time on, I knew that I would live. I felt a release.

This seems so simplistic, but it was life-changing for me. I had known that God was all powerful, but now I knew that it was not for His greater glory for me to die. This thought quieted all the loud voices around me. This gentle prompting of the Holy Spirit through that one verse had brought a healing word into my body. I received it, though it was then only a tiny seed of faith. It was planted in a fertile heart. I have since learned that this was a "rhema" word of God, a spoken word that the Spirit of God quickens in our heart, which is meant for us to be received for a particular situation. This answer was confirmed in my heart with a release of peace: *"For you shall go out with joy, and be led forth with peace..."* (Isaiah 55:12). The symptoms did not change outwardly, but in my heart I knew that I was healed.

The test came one night shortly thereafter, while I was lying awake in my bed. I sensed the presence of death enter my room. My husband was sound asleep next to me and never stirred. It was quiet in the house. I was pleasantly surprised by the words that flowed from my heart, " O death, where is thy sting? Death is swallowed up in victory!" Hallelujah! I rejoiced, realizing that death could not touch me because I was in my Father's hand and Jesus had paid the price for my healing on the cross. I had feared death when I was a child suffering many years with asthma and allergies, but now the presence of death was gone from my life.

That night was a significant obstacle overcome in my journey to wellness. My life was being reestablished upon the truth of what the covenant holds that Jesus made with us. I continued to pray. I found a book about fasting and felt peace about following this regimen. I knew that it was biblical, so I took one day at a time. At the end of three weeks, I awoke one day feeling that I should eat something light. The growths had been reduced by about seventy-five percent in that short of time. Allergies and asthma were gone. The fast had cleansed my body of many things. Over the next few months, the growths continued to diminish and completely disappear. I kept reminding myself of the scripture that God gave me.

There were spiritual concepts that I was made aware of throughout this time. Mark 11:25-26 says, *"And whenever you stand praying, if you have anything against anyone, forgive him, that your Father in heaven may also forgive you your trespasses. But if you do not forgive, neither will your Father in heaven forgive your trespasses."* I hadn't realized that my heart was hurting from unforgiveness, resentment and bitterness that were hidden way down deep. I thought that I had forgiven people in my life that had hurt me, but when I spoke about them, I could only recall the pain they caused and unkind words they had spoken many years before. The Lord showed me that I truly needed to forgive and let go of the events of the past and even reach out in kindness and prayer for these people who had offended me over the years. God is thorough in His approach to bringing us to wholeness in our body, soul, and mind. He guided me through the process of forgiveness, which removed any foothold or defilement that the enemy could have on me or those around me.

Besides these deep issues, I have come to realize that I must keep my eyes on Jesus, the author and finisher of my faith. I had made the mistake of believing in and rehearsing the symptoms. I felt the lumps/growths to see each day how much they had grown. I have learned instead to speak God's Word with my mouth and believe in my heart the promises that He has given to me. I had listened to the faith teachers, but then I would quickly doubt what they said.

I have come to believe and trust in the only source of Truth-that is Jesus Christ, the Living Word of God. The Bible tells us that it is "vain" to trust in man and in Jeremiah it says that *"cursed is the man who trusts in man, and makes flesh his arm, and whose heart depart from the Lord."* (Jeremiah 17:5)

It is *"impossible to please God without faith"* (Hebrews 11:6). *"We wrestle not against flesh and blood, but against ... spiritual powers"* so our weapons must be spiritual when we fight a spiritual battle with a spiritual enemy (Ephesians 6:12).

We would be wise to inquire of the Lord the way David did in the Old Testament, when he was to face a battle. He waited on the Lord and would get the strategy before he went charging into the battle. God knows the battle and He has a higher perspective than us. We should ask Him for the "rhema" word (the strategy) for each battle that we face. This doesn't just apply to healing. We will have a lot more success if we first ask God what we should speak.

Jesus did what He saw His Father doing and He said what His Father said. We would be much wiser and more successful when we follow the example that Jesus gave by following the Father's Words.

CHAPTER 10

CONCLUSION

For there is no partiality with God (Romans 2:11). God does not have favorites in His Kingdom. Many wonder "can I tap into the healings and miracles of Jesus." You can! There needs to a be a hunger and a pressing in for the truth of God's word. Many believers are feeling oriented or glued to the natural realm. Many separate the spiritual and natural realms by their beliefs and corresponding actions. This needs to stop, to create an atmosphere for the miraculous. We have to be people that align our life with the Word, regardless of the circumstances. Don't be moved by what you see or feel as much as being moved by what God's Word says regarding your circumstances. This is how victories and breakthroughs occur.

Your feelings will at times let you down if you are controlled by emotions. Paul said in Romans 1:9 that he served God with his spirit. He did not serve God by his feelings or I guarantee you he would have never accomplished the great things he accomplished for the Kingdom.

Here are some neat things to keep in mind. Notice what Paul said in Romans 12:3, *"For I say, through the grace given to me, to everyone who is among you, not to think of himself more highly than he ought to think, but to think soberly, as God has dealt to each one a measure of faith."* A few things stick out in this verse. One is grace! Keep in mind every blessing or gift, even our health comes by God's grace. What is one of the best ways as followers of Jesus to tap into this grace? Humility! That is the second thing we pick up in this verse. Humility in all areas of our life can set us up for the grace of God, miracles, signs, wonders, blessings and so much more. Both 1 Peter 5:5 and James 4:6 says, *"God resists the proud, but He gives His grace to the humble."* When I started learning this principal of true biblical humility in 1998, the healings, signs, wonders, miracles, favor, blessings, etc all went to a whole new level. I wrote about it in my book *Humility The Hidden Key to Walking in Signs and Wonders.*

Finally, notice that God has dealt to each person a measure of faith. What have you done with your measure of faith? Stewardship of your faith is important if you want your faith to work properly. You can grow, exercise and strengthen your faith in many ways. Many never go anywhere with the faith they were given. That is each person's choice where and how far they go with their faith. Why not go all out with the word being your guide?

Faith pleases God (Hebrews 11:6). Faith helps you overcome the world (1 John 5:4-5). Walk by faith rather than reacting to negative circumstances or the five physical senses (2 Corinthians 5:7). Many feel it is trials that will strengthen their faith. If that is the case then we would all be spiritual giants by now. It is not reality! Without having and exercising faith going through trials many have their measure of faith shipwrecked. Faith increases and comes by hearing God's Word and praying in tongues (Romans 10:17 & Jude vs 20). Faith has to be a foundation in every area of our lives (Hebrews 6:1). There have been exceptions to the rules. People have had miracles and healings without overcoming the roadblocks in their lives, but do not live your life by the exceptions. Live it by the Word. That is when you will see healings and miracles consistently!

Jesus said in Mark 11:22, *"have faith in God."* The original Greek actually words it this way, "Have the Faith of God." What is easier, to try to work up your faith or to have the faith of God? It's yours! It's available! Don't be influenced by Greek philosophy that has crept into our western form of Christianity, but begin to adventure out into the deep with faith in God. Do not let religious tradition be your guide unless it lines up with His Word. Quit settling for second best. Began standing up for what rightfully belongs to you in Christ.

Do not settle for anything less than His ultimate best for your life and health. Understanding we need to be balanced spirit, soul and body will help us see there are things we are responsible to do while working in partnership with the Jesus and the Holy Spirit. Thank God, His grace is there to help out. There are natural laws and there are spiritual laws. Getting a knowledge of both realms helps a person to be balanced and walk in divine health. You can overcome the roadblocks to healing and health with Jesus living on the inside. Time to get after it, my friend!

Mark Anderson Ministries

Vision:

Reaching the unreached, telling the untold, churching the unchurched and training Christians to reach the unreached.

How:

Through open-air campaigns, ministry training conferences, women's conferences (with Sharmila Anderson), planting churches, supporting national ministry leaders, orphanages, literature, CD distribution and contemporary gospel music.

Main Focus:

Rural and unreached areas.

Mark Anderson has been evangelizing, conducting campaigns, singing and planting churches since 1978. Over 200,000 people have already responded to Christ in his overseas campaigns. Churches have been planted from campaigns in India and Bulgaria. Mark has also helped pioneer churches in Canada and the United States.

Mark and his wife, Sharmila, travel together, fulfilling the Great Commission. Sharmila is also a very gifted teacher. Her main area of ministry has been training women to be all they can be in Christ.

To have Mark & Sharmila Anderson come speak in your area or for more information about Mark Anderson Ministries and a list of Mark's books and teaching CDs, please contact them at:

Mark Anderson Ministries
P.O. Box 66
Cody, WY 82414-0066 USA

www.markandersonministries.com
E-mail us at: goodnews@vcn.com
Phone: 307-587-0408

For other books by Mark Anderson, please visit their website:
www.markandersonministries.com/store

FOREWORD BY RANDY CLARK

HUMILITY

THE HIDDEN KEY TO WALKING
IN SIGNS AND WONDERS

MARK R. ANDERSON

Humility: The Hidden Key to Walking in Signs and Wonders

By Mark R. Anderson

published by Destiny Image 2010

Humility is the basis for spiritual and personal breakthrough—no matter your present circumstances. A fresh look at a trait that God welcomes and richly rewards.

As an evangelist in the United States and to Third World countries, author Mark Anderson has observed first-hand how pride can destroy people and churches, while humility can revive and refresh people—and energize and expand even a fledgling ministry.

When pride comes, then comes shame; but with the humble is wisdom (Proverbs 11:2 NKJV).

Humility The Hidden Key to Walking in Signs and Wonders reveals the conflict between arrogance and humility and explores the fruits of this often-neglected but wholly vital virtue.

"The enemy would love for us to neglect humility because of its importance in ushering in the greatest move of God this world has seen," writes the author, who has spent 34 years sharing the gospel worldwide.

> *"This book helps you navigate your life between blatant pride and false humility helping you recognize what true humility looks like...The book is like a diamond in that humility is the diamond, and Mark helps us see all the various facets of the diamond, and there were many, all of which I found very helpful...*
>
> *Humility the Hidden Key to Walking in Signs and Wonders, is the best book I have ever read on humility, and reveals the importance of humility's relationship to spiritual breakthrough, and revival."*

-Randy Clark

You can tap into
Christ's
Healing
Power

Mark R. Anderson

You Can Tap into Christ's Healing Power

By Mark R. Anderson

published by Mark Anderson Ministries 2004

Miracles and healings do not have to be a rarity in your life or the life of any Spirit-filled or Spirit-led believer. By understanding your God-given authority and how to partner with the Holy Spirit, You can tap into Christ's healing power!

Christ made a show of the enemy openly. You can enforce what He accomplished 2,000 years ago. Sometimes faith is a fight. Learn how to stand for what rightfully belongs to you in Christ. Learn how your words shape and affect the way you live your life.

By understanding something that the children of Israel understood, you can create an atmosphere conducive for the Holy Spirit to move in power. You can literally affect the spiritual realm, releasing Christ's healing power in this physical realm. Learn the role humility will play in the healing ministry in these last days.

"Healing the sick was front and center in Jesus ministry. Mark Anderson has years of practical experience in seeing people receive miraculous healing through faith in Christ. His book You Can Tap Into Christ's Healing Power lays a foundation for healing and sets an atmosphere where miracles can easily be received. This teaching is for those who need healing for themselves, as well as for the one who wants to minister God's healing life to others."

Evangelist Peter Youngren
St. Catherines, Ontario, Canada

SOUL WINNING

GOD'S HEARTBEAT

Soul Winning: God's Heartbeat

By Mark R. Anderson

Published by Mark Anderson Ministries 2000

Do you have the desire to reach the lost? Then this book is for you. It includes discussion of:

Witnessing with a passion for souls

Overcoming the fear of witnessing

Successful evangelism keys

Prayerful spiritual warfare and insight into the spirit realm

Saying the right things at the right time

The importance of follow-up

Being a biblical witness with signs and wonders following

The
Progression
of the
Religious Spirit

By Mark R. Anderson

The Progression of the Religious Spirit

By Mark R. Anderson

Published by Mark Anderson Ministries 2001

Jesus warned His close disciples of the negative fruit of the religious spirit. How much more do we need to heed the master's warning today and guard our hearts from an ungodly religious spirit? This book provides an in-depth study of Mark 7:1-13, including:

How the religious spirit begins

Finding fault: The first seed of the religious spirit

Pride and false humility

Holding onto man-made traditions

Laying aside the commands of God

OTHER BOOKS HIGHLY RECOMMENDED BY MARK & SHARMILA

Schizophrenic God? Finding Reality in Conflict, Confusion, and Contradiction

By Steve C. Shank, Boulder, Colorado

published by Destiny Image

Schizophrenic God? is a close look at fate and free will. Has God predetermined everything that happens in your life, or do your own free-will decisions help determine your destiny? You will be challenged to rethink the assumptions you have made about God, which brings comfort and empowerment in the truths of a good God, human choice, and the prayer of faith that changes things. Rest assured—you do not serve a schizophrenic Father

Order from our online bookstore
www.markandersonministries.com/store

Christianity Unshackled

by Harold Eberle Yakima, Washington

published by Destiny Image

"*...Christianity Unschackled is timely and provocative in all the right ways. I read this manuscript with excitement as I can see that God is about to use Harold once again to challenge accepted norms and bring us into a deeper Kingdom experience. This book probes deeply...*"

Bill Johnson, Author of *When Heaven invades Earth*, Senior Pastor of Bethel Church- Redding, CA

"*Christianity Unschackled is a refreshing read for anyone searching for truth in the context of how history shapes our thinking today. An informative and inspiring book to gain a biblical world-view...*" Larry Kreider

Has "Western thought" kept the Church in bondage? This book will give you a Christian worldview upon which you can solidly build your life and confidently make future decisions. You will have a worldview that will hold up against the most fearsome attacks of atheists. You will clearly see a worldview that answers the questions of today's society. And, perhaps most importantly, you will have a worldview that opens your heart and mind to a God who is willing to walk with you and act on your behalf.

Order from our online bookstore
www.markandersonministries.com/store